THE VINTNER'S
APPRENTICE

QUARRY

This beautiful vineyard in the Barossa Valley of Australia is part of today's "New World" of winemaking, where science and the role of the winemaker are more often emphasized than in the "Old World" of Europe where tradition and the role of terroir lead.

PART I:
PLANNING THE VINEYARD

professing to make fine East Coast U.S. wines where none had gone before, and his Benmarl Vineyards got a lot of attention for his particular ability to proselytize and charm at the same time and for his brilliantly creative "Société des Vignerons" that brought Manhattan's wine elite to our door.

When there wasn't a steady stream of East Coast vintners at our dinner table, from Charles Fournier (of the now defunct Gold Seal Winery) to Walter Taylor (scion of the Taylor Wine Company and founder of Bully Hill Vineyards), I found myself in the cellar with the likes of Alexis Lechine (importer, author), Emil Peynaud (Université de Bordeaux), and Peter Sichel (of Blue Nun fame and whose family owned Château Palmer). By then I was hooked.

And ready to expand my horizons. While we experimented with grape varieties that would grow in the harsh New York winters, great things were happening to the west in California. My favorite sporting events were tastings, pitting the likes of Team Mondavi Valley Floor Cabernet Sauvignon against Team Mayacamus Mountain Grown Cabernet. In a slight variation on train spotting, my greatest thrill during those years was a lunch at Freemark Abby's restaurant, identifying legendary figures such as Mike Grgrich and Louis Martini at a table nearby.

It would seem natural that my next move would take me to California, but the lore of fate, family, and my desire to master the *terroir* of a region led me instead on a quest to find the best grape-growing region on the East Coast. This journey ultimately led me to the tiny village of Chadds Ford in southeastern Pennsylvania, where I would spend the next twenty-nine years building the Chaddsford Winery, refining my craft, and satisfying a wellspring of passion to understand my own dirt, my rain, my sun, my wines. Above all, I wanted to make something uniquely Mid-Atlantic, USA, and delicious.

Today, living this life of wine still thrills and fascinates me and drives me toward the next harvest, knowing that it will be like the most amazing Christmas morning, surrounded by packages of possibilities all being opened at the same time. As you read these chapters about what it takes to grow grapes and make wine, about the lifestyle involved, you will see this same passion presented in many different ways, in many different voices.

The good news is that it's not that hard to make drinkable wine. The bad news is that there is no one way to make wine. In this book, in any book, I cannot give you step-by-step directions. I can tell you what's involved and what you need to know and how to find out more. And I can expose you to wine masters who kindly relate their stories and share their understanding about selecting sites and planting vineyards, about harvesting and processing grapes, about cellar work and aging wines, about how to make critical decisions and how to avoid problems. You will find that they do not work with a recipe, but rather react to challenges unique to any given region and vintage.

Author Eric Miller and his wife, Lee Miller, founded the Chaddsford Winery in 1982 and together built it into Pennsylvania's largest and most recognized winery. It is widely respected by consumers and critics alike for its high quality, premium regional wines.

I hope my words and their stories will ignite your passion and encourage you to the next step, whatever that may be. But always, keep that glass in your hand.

ERIC MILLER

I GREW UP IN WINE AND HAVE LIVED MOST OF MY LIFE IN WINE. MY FATHER WAS AN ARTIST WHO WAS HOPELESSLY ROMANCED BY WINE, SO I DIDN'T REALLY HAVE A CHANCE FOR A NONALCOHOLIC CHILDHOOD. GROWING UP IN HARTSDALE, NEW YORK, I LOVED TO PLAY A GAME AT DINNERTIME WHERE MY DAD WOULD BLINDFOLD MY BROTHER AND ME AND OFFER US A SMALL TASTE OF WINE. BY THE AGE OF EIGHT, I HAD GRADUATED FROM IDENTIFYING WHETHER A WINE WAS FROM BURGUNDY OR BORDEAUX AND WAS ON TO THE GREATER CHALLENGE OF TELLING WHETHER IT WAS RED OR WHITE.

INTRODUCTION

By the age of thirteen, I had begun our family's annual uprooting to new schools in new countries. We were living in the small town of Saint-Romain, Burgundy, where I made the delicious discovery that the ancient Roman sewer system under the main street opened into most of the wine cellars in town. It made perfect sense that everyone I knew either exported wine, made wine, or made barrels for wine.

Those years in France exposed me to wine and food in the way only the French can do it. Later, while living in England (during what I call "the boarding school era"), where there were no beautiful vineyards or romantic cellars, I turned my attention to learning about the wine trade, as only the

British can do it. With my modest understanding of French wine regions and wine types, I became judge and jury of illegal blending practices. I'll never forget discovering the guilty logic of a rogue bottler saying, "One man's Châteauneuf du Pape is another man's Nuit St. George." How could they say Pinot Noir tastes like Syrah and Grenache?

At the age of nineteen, back in the United States, bored with college, desperately trying to avoid getting a job, I ended up working the steep hillsides of my father's newly planted vineyard in the Hudson Valley. I found myself alternating between jeans and tuxedo but always with a glass of wine in hand. Dad was quite an upstart,

From his earliest days, author Eric Miller has been surrounded by wine, grapes, vineyards, and wineries. Wine is both his vocation and his lifelong avocation.

Growing grapes and making wine, especially great wine, is not an easy endeavor. And most books available on these subjects are extremely technical, almost taking the fun out of the process. *The Vintner's Apprentice* is the first book on winemaking that I have ever read that keeps the romance of wine balanced with the technical aspects of this art. The proliferation of vineyards and wineries in the "New World' is unprecedented. In the United States alone there are now 6,000 wineries, which is up from a mere 200 forty years ago when I first met Eric.

While Eric has written extensively about the art and process of winemaking, he has also interviewed winemakers from South Africa, France, the United States, Italy, Chile, and Germany, which gives the reader great insight into winemaking around the world. If you are like Eric and me, who have found our passion for growing grapes, making wine, and (of course) drinking it, and are considering this kind of lifestyle for yourself, you must begin your journey by reading the stories of how the great winemakers of the world began their journey. You read real stories from real winemakers, the up side and the down side, while always maintaining a sense of humor and enthusiasm, supplemented with beautiful photography. This should be everyone's go-to book to understand where to plant grapes (soil types, weather and wine conditions), what grapes to plant (*Vitis vinifera*, *Vitis labrusca*, hybrids), and what you can expect to achieve in the final product.

The book is full of fascinating and useful information in a down-to-earth approach with such things as The Winemaker's Tool Box, The Vintner's Marketplace, and solving winemaking problems. *The Vintner's Apprentice* even tells you how wine barrels and corks are made and how they help in aging. The joy of harvest, the excitement, emotion, and exhaustion of crush time, to the disappointment of some harvests with the threat of rain, frost, or hail—it's all here.

So how do winemakers make wine? From Missouri to St. Emilion, France, from the Old World to the New World, everyone has a unique take on the process. This book is all about the journey of grapes from the vineyard through the winery to the wine on your dinner table! Eric Miller makes this wine journey easy, simple to understand, and enjoyable, and I am honored and proud to introduce this book to you.

KEVIN ZRALY
Author and educator, Windows on the World Complete Wine Course

FOREWORD

MY FIRST VISIT TO A WINERY AND VINEYARD WAS TO BENMARL, THE HIGHLY ACCLAIMED WINERY IN THE HUDSON VALLEY OF NEW YORK RUN BY ERIC MILLER'S FAMILY, A DAY THAT LIVES INGRAINED IN MY MEMORY. I SAW ROW UPON ROW OF BEAUTIFUL VINES RISING UP AND DIPPING DOWN THE VALLEY'S FLOOR. I SAW THE BIG METAL TANKS AND WOODEN OAK BARRELS. SINCE THAT DAY I HAVE WANTED TO PLANT VINES AND MAKE WINE. ERIC HELPED ME PLANT MY FIRST VINEYARD WHEN I WAS 23, AND HE HELPED ME PLANT MY MOST RECENT ONE FOUR YEARS AGO. HE HAS ALWAYS BEEN THERE FOR ANY OF MY "FARMING QUESTIONS," AND NOW HE HAS WRITTEN THE BEST BOOK ON GRAPE GROWING AND WINEMAKING FOR ANSWERING YOUR QUESTIONS.

INTERVIEWS WITH THE MASTERS

CONTENTS

TO MY WIFE AND CO-AUTHOR
LEE MILLER, BECAUSE THERE
ARE THOUSANDS OF WONDERFUL
WINES I WANT TO TASTE AND
SMELL AND FEEL, BUT ONLY
ONE LEE.

First published in the United States
of America by Quarry Books, a member of
Quayside Publishing Group
100 Cummings Center
Suite 406-L
Beverly, Massachusetts 01915-6101
Telephone: (978) 282-9590
Fax: (978) 283-2742
www.quarrybooks.com

Library of Congress
Cataloging-in-Publication Data

Miller, Eric, 1949-
Vintner's apprentice : the insider's guide to
the art and craft of wine making, taught by
the masters / Eric Miller.
    p. cm.
 Includes bibliographical references and
index.

JULY 2011

1. Wine and wine making. 2. Vintners—
Interviews. I. Title.

TP548.M6265 2011
663'.2—dc22
                                    2010029010

ISBN-13: 978-1-59253-657-3
ISBN-10: 1-59253-657-3

10 9 8 7 6 5 4 3 2 1

Design: Paul Burgess: Burge Agency
Artwork: Peter Usher: Burge Agency
Front cover photos: shutterstock; Brian
Piper Photography; Eric Miller/Chaddsford
Winery; shutterstock; University of Min-
nesota, David L. Hansen
Spine photo: Stone Hill Winery
Back cover photos: Serge Bois Prévot;
istockphoto.com; Penfolds

Printed in China

BEVERLY MASSACHUSETTS

QUARRY BOOKS

THE INSIDER'S
GUIDE TO THE ART
AND CRAFT OF WINE
MAKING, TAUGHT BY
THE MASTERS

THE VINTNER'S
APPRENTICE ERIC MILLER

WINEMAKERS ARE, BY NATURE, ARTISTIC INDIVIDUALISTS WHO WILL ARGUE INDEFINITELY (WHILE SHARING A BOTTLE OF WINE) ABOUT THE IMPORTANCE OF CLUSTER THINNING IN THE VINEYARD OR WHETHER A PARTICULAR WINE HAS *BRETTANOMYCES*. BUT FEW WILL DIFFER ON THE SIGNIFICANCE OF WHERE THE GRAPE IS GROWN. WORLD-RENOWNED VITICULTURE AUTHORITY DR. RICHARD SMART OF AUSTRALIA SUMS IT UP QUITE SUCCINCTLY: "SITE SELECTION," HE SAID, "IS MORE IMPORTANT THAN SPOUSAL SELECTION."

CHAPTER 1:
SELECTING A SITE

I got my first lesson on vineyard site location from my father the first time I was in Burgundy on the way back from boarding school. He picked me up at the train station in Dijon and pulled off the road just before Beaune, where he excitedly pointed out the "golden slope," the famous Côte d'Or. "Look," he said, gesturing upward to the rising vineyards of Nuits-Saint-Georges, "those wines that come from the vines up on the slope are worth three times more than the wines from the bottom."

It was December and the vines were dormant, bare, bent, and brown, but I could still tell something was different. On the high slopes were neatly cultivated rows of perfect vines, beautifully laid stone walls, and wrought iron gates. Lower down were ramshackle rows of muddy vineyards marked by old wooden signs and posts.

The reality is that there is no one element, or mix of elements, that make up a perfect wine-growing site, whether you are sitting in a 600-year-old abbey overlooking a world-renowned vineyard or staring at your own "back 40" dreaming about planting a few vines. But over centuries of trial and error, some places have proven to consistently grow good grapes, the type that allow winemakers to strut their stuff in the marketplace. How?

One answer can be found in the juxtaposition of soils, climate, and topography that have come together on that particular site, a relationship that is often referred to as *terroir*. (For more about terroir, see "A Tale of Two Vineyards" later in this chapter) Over time, these factors will determine not only the vigor and productivity of the grapevines but also the eventual quality of the wines made from them.

CLIMATE AND WEATHER

Climate is complex; it includes sunlight, temperature, wind, rainfall, and other occasional acts of nature such as hail (ouch!) and snow.

Sunlight provides energy and heat for the plant to grow. Sun warms the earth and the dormant brown wood of the vines, transforms pregnant buds into green growth and fruit, fuels photosynthesis, and triggers the vine to shift its energies and nutrients from one part of the plant to another. But excess sun can actually burn the plant and evaporate needed moisture in the soil.

Temperature in a particular region margins the all-important growing season. The minimal season, from the last frost of spring to the first leaf-killing frost of fall, is

With unlimited melt from the Andes Mountains providing irrigation, Argentina's arid Mendoza district is becoming increasingly recognized for its ability to grow striking Malbec grapes and wine.

These mature Pinot Noir grapevines on the author's Miller Estate Vineyard in southeastern Pennsylvania are rooted some 30 feet (9.1 m) deep into well-drained gravely silt loam soils.

about 165 days between 50°F and 90°F (10°C and 32°C). Vines luxuriate between 70°F and 85°F (21°C and 29°C), given sufficient moisture. The dead zone, when a vine simply shuts down and stops most functions, including ripening, is somewhere around 95°F (35°C). On the other end of the scale, vines lose their leaves when they hit freezing temperatures at 32°F (0°C), retreating to dormancy until the temperatures rise again in spring. In the interim, a deep snow cover can insulate vines from killing winter cold.

Wind movement, or airflow, dries excess moisture in the soil and keeps cold temperatures and killing frosts from settling around the vines. It also helps dry the vine to discourage pests and diseases from making a home there. But if air speed is too high or too strong, it can break or desiccate the vine's shoots and leaves.

Moisture allows nutrient transport from the roots up through the exposed parts of the vine. Most regions depend on moderate rainfall throughout the growing season, but not so much that humidity supports molds, pests, and disease. Too much moisture can also drown the vine's roots, particularly in heavy wet soil that doesn't drain well. In arid regions, lack of sufficient rainfall can be adjusted through the use of irrigation.

TOPOGRAPHY AND ELEVATION

Hills, valleys, slopes, and swales—topography is simply the lay of the land. Its various features provide opportunity for sun exposure, air movement, and water drainage.

It affects temperature zones; for instance, warm air zones can be found partway up a slope, before the air chills at higher elevation, inverts, and falls back down into the valley floor below. The altitude of the site is very significant in its relationship to surrounding features. With elevations higher than where heavy frosts settle, vines will retain their leaves for a longer growing season.

SOILS / DIRT

Today's soil quality and substance was determined more than 8,000 years ago during Earth's last ice age, when retreating glaciers shoved mountaintops from northern Spain to France's west coast and the ocean was just receding from the center of North America. In the vineyard, the soil's job is to anchor the plant and provide most

The "left bank" and "right bank" of the River Gironde that flows through Bordeaux, France, have very different characteristics. The left bank vineyards are large, with prestigious châteaux, while right bank vineyards are much smaller, sometimes enclosed by walls (*clos*); the terroir is different as well. The left bank lies on gravels that were washed down the river a millennia ago from the distant Pyrenees, while the right bank lies on soil that contains clay enriched with iron.

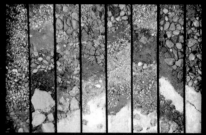

Core samples, taken in the town of Graves, France, from the extremely gravelly left bank of the Gironde River. Although this area was once a mosquito-infested swamp, when drained it became home to more classified Bordeaux châteaux than any other part of France.

A roadside cut of typical soil in the town of Frontenac, France, on the right bank of the Gironde River, where heavy clay sits on top of an extremely well-drained cracked layer of limestone.

of its nutritional needs. Grapevines prosper in an amazing range of soils as long as they are well drained: gravel and limestone are among the favored; soils with heavy clay are among the most difficult. A pH of 5.5 to 7.0 seems to be ideal, with minimal nitrogen levels and a smattering of other minerals such as potassium, iron, boron, calcium, phosphorus, magnesium, zinc, copper, and molybdenum.

RELATIONSHIPS AND RELATIVITY

Like most things in life, vineyard conditions are relative. You can grow great grapes on moisture-retentive soils if the growing season is dry. The thrill of an early start to the growing season may be countered by a late spring frost that zaps the tender green growth, seriously damaging crop level. In regions where the season would normally be too short, days either have longer sunny periods or nights are warm enough to keep the vine cranking after dark. And so on. The successful winegrower will not only understand these intricacies and how they affect the vines but will also move on to other relationships that play a part in the end goal of making top-quality wines. Among the most important will be selection of grape varieties to plant on the site and the cultural practices employed in maintaining it.

I NTERVIEW WITH:
LUCIE MORTON, VITICULTURIST

LUCIE MORTON AND I STARTED WORKING IN THE EASTERN UNITED STATES WINE INDUSTRY ABOUT THE SAME TIME, IN THE EARLY 1970S. SHE WAS FUN, LOVED WINE, WAS WILLING TO RIDE ON THE BACK OF MY OLD BMW MOTORCYCLE, AND KNEW WHERE ALL THE EXCITING VINEYARDS WERE IN THE REGION.

At the time, she was traipsing across the United States, discovering infant and pre-natal wineries with Leon Adams, the author of *Wines of America*. Leon was, she says, "a turbo-energetic, stocky, beret-capped, bow-tied, talkative, and abrupt septuagenarian who did not at all fit my preconceptions of a wine connoisseur. But," she continues, "he was determined to visit all the wineries of North America, and I was determined to visit all the vineyards." Today Lucie is a well-respected international viticultural consultant and lecturer whose specialties include grapevine identification, grapevine rootstock selection, analysis of the relationship between viticultural practices and wine quality, and new vineyard establishment. She has consulted for vineyards up and down the East Coast, as well as vineyards in California, Oregon, France, New Zealand, Australia, Chile, and Crete.

LUCIE, TELL ME IN YOUR OWN WORDS WHAT YOU DO FOR THE WINE INDUSTRY.

I am what you call an independent viticulturist, but mostly you could say that I'm a problem solver. I consider myself a student of vines. So when vines are not behaving according to plan, people call me in to see what might be going wrong. Because I've been a student of vines for so long, I'm able to rule out a lot of things. On the positive side, we are always looking to coax the best wine out of the vineyards.

HOW DID YOU BECOME A WORLD-TRAVELING AUTHORITY ON VINEYARDS?

I guess you could say it started when my father asked me to plant a vineyard on the banks of the Potomac River in Virginia. At the time, I knew absolutely nothing about vines or vineyards. In many ways I've always thought that the fact that I went into this with no knowledge at all about grape growing has in the end been a bit of a benefit. Here I was a young, college-educated person who didn't have a clue what I wanted to do—but I was very enthusiastic, and here was this great opportunity, so I just had to go out and, well, learn. And then I got some lucky breaks.

Viticultural consultant Lucie Morton enjoys vineyard consulting because each site is so unique. "Each time I visit a vineyard, it's like starting all over again," she says.

The 28-acre (11.3 ha) vineyard of the famous Château Petrus of Pomerol, Bordeaux, breaks many of the rules used in selecting new vineyard sites today. Nevertheless, it is one of the most highly rated and expensive wines in the world.

LIKE WHAT?

The thing that really gave me a leg up was meeting two key people in Maryland: Philip Wagner of Boordy Vineyards and Hamilton Mowbray of Montbray Wine Cellars. Phil was the person who first introduced French-American hybrid grapes to the United States, and Ham had started planting vinifera varieties like Cabernet. Then my next break was that we had a friend and neighbor, Caroline Guest, wife of Ambassador Raymond Guest, who was French, and it turns out her good friend was Lilliane de Rothschild at Château Lafite—so she arranged for me to go pick grapes there! And that eventually led me to study at the École Nationale Supérieure Agronomique de Montpellier, pretty much the world's best-known viticulture school, where I became the first American ever to do the Montpellier program. After that, there was nowhere to go but up!

WHAT MAKES A GOOD HOME FOR THE VINE?

I wish more people consulted me at the beginning so I could help them pick the ideal site. Often, I'm handed a vineyard on a site already established and have to make the best of it. But in the big picture, the right site is the single most important "you can't fix it later" factor in vineyard development. But then again, a majority of vineyards have some site factors that are suboptimal and there are viticultural strategies to deal with these—drainage tiles, compost, rootstock selection, chain saws for cutting down trees. It's a critical factor

The Boxwood Winery vineyard in Middleburg, Virginia, was carefully laid out to conform to the land, summer sunlight, and prevailing winds.

for me that the vineyard site be well away from trees. *Trees* rhymes with *disease*. Trees make undesirable shade, which creates unhealthy microclimate conditions. Trees harbor harmful visible and invisible pests from birds to berry moths to yellows, causing phytoplasma and Pierce's disease, causing bacteria.

WHAT OTHER FACTORS ARE SIGNIFICANT IN SITE SELECTION?

The truisms are generally true. Grapes like good relative elevation and well-drained soil. The idea is to avoid areas where cold air pools and creates frost and freeze hazards. And to avoid wet feet, where vine roots have a hard time breathing. Of course, there are always exceptions to the rules, like Château Petrus, which lies in flat terrain and heavy clay—but then again, Bordeaux is a place with a proven track record that trumps truisms.

A TALE OF TWO VINEYARDS

Sometimes there is a thin line between success and failure in a vineyard. Lucie Morton has seen plenty of both in her long career as an international viticultural consultant.

SUCCESS RIGHT FROM THE START

Lucie Morton worked with Ed Boyce and Sarah O'Herron from day one to find the perfect site for their dream vineyard in Maryland. They did not have an existing family farm they insisted on working with, but—with the kind of foresight she associates with success—gave her free rein to find the right location. After a two-year search she chose the 146-acre (59 ha) property that eventually became their Black Ankle Vineyard, settling on these desirable site features:

Site altitude was 600 feet (182 m), and, importantly, was higher than the surrounding land.

It had two distinct ridges on either side of a little valley, providing excellent air and soil drainage.

Slopes were gentle, important for tractor safety and allowing easy planting and harvesting.

The orientation of the site was such that vine rows could run north-to-south, maximizing sunlight and photosynthesis.

The western slope got hot afternoon sun exposure, making it ideal for growing the red varieties Cabernet Sauvignon and Syrah; white varieties including Albariño, Grüner Veltliner, and Chardonnay were planted on a north-facing slope with less direct sun.

Today, Black Ankle Vineyard has 40 acres (16.2 ha) of wine grapes under cultivation, and Ed and Sarah have received very flattering reviews for the wines they produce there, wines they feel "express the unique flavors and atmosphere of the land on which they are grown."

NEAR DISASTERS

But things don't always go that well. Lucie has also been hired to evaluate a number of sites that turned out to be unsuitable for grape growing. Among the problems she's encountered:

Undesirable soil makeup

Unsuitable elevation

Lowlands with no air movement

Sites surrounded by trees

Too much water; bad drainage

Sometimes things start out looking bad, then finish with a happy ending. Lucie writes, "There was a prospective vintner with a site I thought wasn't high enough and I told him he just didn't have enough elevation to do a vineyard. But then I got to the site and realized the field was a topographical breezeway, which is very good! So we dug more than thirty pits and found that the soils were fine, and ended up dividing the vineyard into two big blocks in order to avoid a riparian swale that ran through the field. Today it is a beautiful model vineyard!"

WHAT DO YOU DO WHEN YOUR CLIENT WANTS TO PLANT ON A SITE THAT YOU KNOW IS A DISASTER?

If a site is really bad, I advise against planting there at all, particularly if it is for a commercial enterprise. But sometimes people do it anyway. So I just try to help them optimize the site by making good choices elsewhere, like in the selection of grape varieties and rootstocks. In the end, if a vineyard I help design does well, most of the credit should go to the owners and their staff.

WHAT ADVICE WOULD YOU GIVE TO A NEW GROWER ABOUT THE SIGNIFICANCE OF A GOOD SITE?

It's not how many acres you have, it's how you use them! Today there is a movement toward closer row spacing and closer vine spacing (higher density plantings) to fully maximize use of a good site—something they have always done in Europe because they recognize how precious good vineyard land is. I'm not sure this has been fully appreciated in "New World" regions until recently. But as land prices continue to go up, it will be, as we're seeing now in California.

Wines from Grands Échezeaux, Burgundy, considered to be among the finest Pinot Noir sites in the world, can draw absolutely exorbitant prices per bottle. At a different vineyard within the same town, the same vintage sells for one-tenth the price.

If you're going to plant a vineyard, be really, really sure! Following your dream is good. Doing it because you inherited your in-laws' farm is not.

I've had to follow that advice myself. Long after my career was launched by planting vines on our family farm, long after we sold it and the vineyard had been pulled out, I was hired by the man who bought it. He asked me to evaluate the advisability of replanting a vineyard there. So I ended up telling him, "I don't know how I ever grew a grape here. This is a terrible site. I don't recommend it. You've got a high water table. You're surrounded by woods. You have the romance of the river, but that's about all you've got going for you. So if I were you I would not plant a single vine." Talk about coming full circle!

This now abandoned vineyard (which was established in the 1970s) is an example of poor site selection. It illustrates that the vines themselves will let you know whether the elevation and water drainage are less than ideal.

I'D BEEN HAVING A PASSIONATE LOVE AFFAIR WITH THE SWEET DESSERT WINES OF PORTUGAL FOR ALMOST TEN YEARS BEFORE I LEARNED THAT ONE OF THE MAIN GRAPE VARIETIES USED IN PORTS IS TOURIGA NACIONAL. LIKEWISE, MOST PEOPLE DON'T KNOW THAT THE CHIANTIS THEY DRINK ARE MOSTLY MADE FROM THE SANGIOVESE GRAPE. ON THE OTHER HAND, VARIETIES SUCH AS CHARDONNAY AND MERLOT HAVE BECOME SO UBIQUITOUS ON WINE LISTS TODAY THAT THEY ARE ALMOST SYNONYMOUS WITH "WHITE WINE" AND "RED WINE," RESPECTIVELY.

CHAPTER 2:
CHOOSING GRAPE VARIETIES

So just what is a grape variety and what is its significance to the winegrower and wine drinker? In its simplest form, a grape variety is a subset of the plant genus *Vitis*. It is how we identify various grapes, and often the name given to the "varietal" wines made from them, such as Pinot Grigio or Cabernet Sauvignon. There are literally thousands of grape varieties growing around the world, but relatively few that are known and grown and recognized worldwide (see "The World's Most Popular Grape Varieties" later in this chapter).

Each grape variety has signature characteristics that will determine which type of wines it is ultimately used for. Thus, choosing precisely which grapes to plant in a vineyard is a complex and far-reaching decision that should be made with the end goal in mind. Which type of wines does the vintner want to make? Dry? Sweet? White? Red? Are the wines being made for personal consumption, to share with friends and family? Or to sell to the public? What is hot in today's marketplace or being talked about as the next "up-and-comer"?

With a clear vision in mind, the vintner can then go on to choose the best grape varieties for the site, based on taste preference, marketing considerations, site conditions, and other important criteria.

In Europe, law or tradition most often rules when it comes to which grape varieties are planted where. In Germany, several varieties are legal, but vignerons in the Mosel Valley tend to use their best sites to grow the traditionally accepted Riesling grape.

PERSONAL PREFERENCE

Any small winery owner can tell you a story about the customer who wants to know how he or she got the peaches or chocolate into the wine. Maybe winemakers do get carried away with descriptors sometimes, but the fact is, wines have an incredible range of smells and flavors that come naturally from the grapes we grow. Thus, if the winemaking goal is to produce a light, fresh, dry red wine with hints of strawberry, the vintner will look for a fruity grape such as Gamay Beaujolais or Grenache or Chambourcin. If the opposite is desired—a big, earthy, full-bodied wine with mouth-searing tannins—king Cabernet or the mighty Nebbiolo might be selected.

Even though the vintner's personal preference is not as significant in a commercial winery selling to the public, the knowledge of what each variety tastes like is—and the more you hone your personal preference—the better your winemaking decisions will be. There is no one simple way to achieve this knowledge, because it is often based on a lifetime of tasting, talking, and experiencing wines at the dinner table every night. Other ways to achieve a perspec-

tive on grape varieties are attending wine classes, joining tasting groups, attending wine conferences, visiting wineries, and reading respected publications, such as Steve Tanzer's *International Wine Cellar*, Robert Parker's *Wine Advocate*, *Decanter* magazine, and *Wine Spectator*, that provide tasting notes, surveying wines by variety, region, and producer.

THE MARKETPLACE

In the world of commercial winemaking, commerce has about 99.9 percent to do with what's grown in the vineyard. It doesn't help to have a cellar full of absolutely charming crisp white wines if the customer wants big, bold, barrel-aged reds. If your vineyard is smack dab in the middle of the Napa Valley you'd be crazy not to grow Cabernet Sauvignon when that's what the region is known for and that's what fetches the most money. Knowing what is currently popular, what's up-and-coming, and most important, what's selling, should play a big part in determining what to plant in the vineyard. Even the greatest winemaker has to sell his work if he wants to stay in business! But every variety may not be appropriate for every site or region.

WINE PRODUCING REGIONS

Many wine-growing regions throughout the world have become known for growing certain grape varieties.

REGION	VARIETY
Burgundy, France	Chardonnay
Vinho Verde, Portugal	Albariño/Alvarinho
Germany	Riesling
New Zealand	Sauvignon Blanc
South Africa	Chenin Blanc/Steen
Barossa Valley, Australia	Shiraz/Syrah
Chianti, Italy	Sangiovese
Piedmonte, Italy	Nebbiolo
Oregon, U.S.	Pinot Noir
Mendoza, Argentina	Malbec
Rioja, Spain	Tempranillo
California, U.S.	Cabernet Sauvignon
Pennsylvania, U.S.	Chambourcin

A one-year-old vine, showing the graft union at the bottom. This is where the rootstock is grafted onto the scion, or fruiting portion of the vine.

CLIMATE AND GROWING CONDITIONS

Each grape variety has its own growing characteristics. Chardonnay, for instance, loses acidity when the weather or climate is too hot. Barbera needs hot weather and a long growing season to reduce its naturally high acidity. Albariño seems to like a moist, sunny climate. Riesling likes cool sunny days and cool nights. Syrah thrives in heat-reflecting stone soils and extremely dry conditions, such as in the northern Rhône Valley, while Garnacha reaches ultimate intensity in Priorato, Spain, where thousands of scraggly draught-stricken vines per hectare might produce one agonized cluster per plant. (Talk about high-priced wines!) Is it any wonder, then, that these, and other varieties, over centuries of trial and error, have come to be associated with certain regions?

TRADITION AND LEGALITIES

Some countries, particularly in Europe, take all the guesswork out of which varieties to plant by legislating exactly which grapes may be grown and must be used in certain regions. In the highly organized wine districts of France, it is illegal to plant and market anything but approved grape varieties. In Champagne, only three varieties may legally be used to make wine: Pinot Noir, Chardonnay, and Pinot Meunier. In Bordeaux, only six red varieties are permitted: Cabernet Sauvignon, Cabernet Franc, Merlot, Petite Verdot, Malbec, and Carmenere.

In other Old World regions, centuries of tradition—rather than strict laws—dictate what is appropriate and acceptable. In Italy's Piedmont region, for instance, Nebbiolo is the red grape of choice, even though you can find plenty of wine made from Barbera and Dolcetto; farther south in Tuscany, it's all about Sangiovese in your Chianti. Such varietal traditions are also beginning to emerge in New World regions such as Mendoza, Argentina, where local preference seems to be for the floral characteristics of Torrontes as the white grape of choice.

Way up north where the summer is short and the winter cold, a select few grape varieties have adapted and make some very good wines. The Alexis Bailly Vineyard in Hastings, Minnesota, lets you know how "the grapes suffer" when you enter the property.

A TALE OF TWO CHARDONNAYS

In many Old World countries, wines are named after their region. One example is in the Chablis region of France, where the grapes must be 100 percent Chardonnay—but you will only see "Chablis" on the label. In other markets, such as the United States, the grape variety name is typically featured on the label. So if the grape is Chardonnay, the label will likely say "Chardonnay," provided the wine meets U.S. labelling laws, which say that the wine must be at least 75 percent of the stated grape in order to use the variety name.

WIDE WORLD OF GRAPE VARIETIES

Grape varieties come in all shapes, sizes, colors, and flavors!

Many wineries choose the grape varieties they plant and the wine varietals they produce based on what they hear from customers in the tasting room—and what they buy!

The Concord grape is pest resistant and cold tolerant and has a powerful fruity smell and flavor profile. It is used to make both grape juice and wine. (Concord is native to the northeastern United States.)

Pinot Noir, from the *Vitis vinifera* family, is often called "the heartbreak grape" or "the Holy Grail." It drives winegrowers mad with the delicacy, foresight, dedication, and luck needed to bring in its ultimate expression.

Norton, also known as Cynthiana, is well adapted to the broad-ranging weather patterns of a continental climate. It is native to the midwestern United States.

La Crescent is a Muscat hybrid with intense fruit, high acidity, moderate disease resistance, and a hardy heritage that has survived an amazing −36°F (−37.8°C) in Minnesota, U.S.

Jon Held, winemaker and general manager at Stone Hill Winery, evaluates clusters of Norton grapes, a variety that is very significant and well adapted to his Missouri climate and clientele. Norton is a native North American species also known as Cynthiana.

INTERVIEW WITH:
JON HELD, STONE HILL WINERY, MISSOURI, UNITED STATES

THERE ARE THE MEDIA STARS IN THE WINE BUSINESS AND THEN THERE ARE THE TRUE HEROES, LIKE JON HELD, WHO GO OUT EVERY DAY TO WORK IN THE VINEYARDS, LABOR ON THE CRUSH PAD, AND CREATE FIRST-RATE WINES AND WINERIES IN PLACES THAT DO NOT HAVE THE GLITZ AND GLAMOUR OF BIG NAME WINE REGIONS.

Jon is the powerhouse who grew a small, respected family business in central Missouri into a highly successful, multiple location winery, yet he somehow finds time to invest in things that will benefit and shape the U.S. wine industry thirty years from now. I got to know him when we shared seats on the USDA-funded Viticulture Consortium, tasked with evaluating and funding grape research across the United States. He passionately supported research into regionally appropriate grape varieties and for funding a collection of Hungarian varieties he hoped would add new genes to the hybridizing pool.

When Jon hosted a Consortium meeting at his family's Stone Hill Winery in recent years, attendees saw and tasted firsthand some amazing varieties few knew were being grown. (This is saying something considering wine is both a vocation and a full-time avocation for most people in the Consortium.) For lunch he showed us a vertical tasting (several different vintages of the same wine sampled in order from youngest to oldest) of Norton. For dinner he served a barrel-aged "Chardonel" (a Chardonnay hybrid). It was exciting, and it gave everyone a broadened view of the grapes and wines of the future.

JON, HOW ARE YOU GROWING GRAPES IN STONE HILL, MISSOURI? ISN'T IT A RELATIVELY COLD CLIMATE?

Stone Hill farms seven vineyards totaling approximately 175 acres (70.8 ha) in central Missouri along the Missouri River. And yes, we do have a very harsh climate with cold, fluctuating winter temperatures. So winter hardiness has historically been the key criteria for selecting varieties to grow here. But there is no question that we have seen a shift in the climate over the past twenty-five years—I remember all frigid temperatures of –20°F (–28.9°C) back in the early 1980s—but for the past several years we have seldom seen below 0°F (–17.8°C).

"Drink the wine you like, not the wine someone tells you to like."

SO WHAT DO YOU GROW THERE? SURELY NOT DELICATE VINIFERA VARIETIES SUCH AS PINOT GRIGIO AND RIESLING.

We have a mixture of native American grapes, French hybrids, and other hybrids. I consider the only commercially viable varieties for our region to be Concord, Catawba, Vidal Blanc, Norton, Vignoles, Cayuga, Traminette, Chambourcin, St. Vincent, and Chardonel. We have other varieties of limited acreage, but these are the main ones.

Until ten years ago, I would not have considered even a trial planting of the mainstream *Vitis vinifera* varieties. Today, I am considering a small planting. Time will tell whether it's economically feasible or not. It's definitely cool to have a hobby vineyard in Missouri with nothing but vinifera varieties, but given our current climatic conditions they are not reliable enough to pay the bank regularly. For the Held family, this is definitely a business—not a hobby!

HOW EXACTLY DID YOU GET INVOLVED IN THIS NON-HOBBY VENTURE?

Where do I begin? I started tagging along with my father in the vineyards around 1965 when I was just seven years old. By the time I was ten, he had me pulling brush beside him as he pruned the vines. By age fourteen, I was driving an old tractor with a sprayer behind it, spraying the vineyards to control fungal diseases. Child labor laws were not a consideration back then!

In the decades before this, the Missouri grape/wine industry consisted primarily of native American varieties such as Concord and Catawba. Then, in 1965, my parents bought the old Stone Hill Winery and began restoring it. In the late 1960s, they started planting a few then "experimental" varieties—Vidal, Seyval, and Chelois. They continued to expand in the 1970s, working in cooperation with the University of Missouri, and by the time I left to study enology and viticulture at California State University, Fresno, in 1976, we had significant acreage of hybrid varieties.

AND THEN YOU RETURNED TO STONE HILL?

I joined the family business in 1983 as vineyard manager and began to increase our plantings. I also became active on the Missouri Grape and Wine Board. The state has done a lot of experimental plantings, including French American hybrids, American interspecific hybrids, German hybrids, Eastern European hybrids, and even a few of the mainstream vinifera varieties. As a result of this continuing research, the varietal makeup of the Missouri grape industry has completely changed during the past fifteen years. Norton has become the most planted variety followed by Chardonel.

TELL ME ABOUT HYBRIDS BRIEFLY. IF THERE'S SO MUCH EXPERIMENTATION GOING ON, HOW DO YOU DECIDE WHICH VARIETIES TO PUT YOUR MONEY ON?

There are a lot of considerations, but the two most important criteria are wine quality and adaptation to the climate. In this "new frontier of grape growing," we have a lot of disease pressure, so we're looking for breeding with disease resistance, and also hardiness. A lot of the new hybrids are 50 percent vinifera grafted onto different rootstocks for more resistance to phylloxera. As the percentage of vinifera increases in some of the newer hybrids, so does the susceptibility to phylloxera; therefore, we need to graft to a resistant rootstock.

THE WORLD'S MOST POPULAR GRAPE VARIETIES

Although there are thousands of grape varieties in the world, relatively few are grown and successfully marketed worldwide. Wine educators often teach classes about "The Big Six" and wine writers like to talk about the "Top Ten." Here is a hybrid list of top international varieties:

Chardonnay

Pinot Gris/Pinot Grigio

Riesling

Sauvignon Blanc

Cabernet Sauvignon

Merlot

Pinot Noir

Syrah/Shiraz

VARIETY IS THE SPICE OF LIFE

Despite the popularity of the top varieties, there is a fascinating and tasty list of wonderful, lesser-known varieties well worth seeking out, including:

Whites: Albariño, Chenin Blanc, Cortese, Gewürztraminer, Grüner Veltliner, Malvasia, Marsanne, Muscat, Palomino, Pinot Blanc, Rousanne, Sémillon, Tocai, Torrontes, Vidal Blanc, Vignoles, Viognier

Reds: Aglianico, Barbera, Cabernet Franc, Carmenere, Chambourcin, Corvino, Dolcetto d'Alba, Gamay Beaujolais, Garnacha/Grenache, Malbec, Mavrotragana, Mourvèdre, Nebbiolo, Nero d'Avola, Norton, Petite Syrah, Petit Verdot, Pinot Meunier, Primativo, Sagrantino, Sangiovese, Tempranillo, Touriga Nacional, Zinfandel

Lower winter temperatures require cold-tolerant grape varieties.

When you consider the issue of quality, you sometimes have to compromise, as with Vignoles. The wine quality is so high it nearly outweighs the viticulture shortcomings. I describe that variety as being like an ex-spouse. Certain qualities you clearly appreciate. But there's a whole bunch of things you would rather live without! Other times, you just roll the dice. The variety Traminette is where we've gambled the most. I probably have one of the biggest plantings in the world, close to 20 acres (8.1 ha).

WHAT IS IT ABOUT THAT GRAPE THAT GIVES YOU THAT KIND OF COURAGE?

Just beautiful chemistry. Great balance. Beautiful flavor.

WHAT ABOUT THE NORTON VARIETAL? YOU'VE MENTIONED IT A LOT; WHAT DO YOU THINK OF ITS POTENTIAL AS AN INTERNATIONAL GRAPE VARIETY?

Well, I don't know about "international best seller" but on a regional basis it does very well and has quite a following. It has become Missouri's most planted variety, but Concord and Catawba wines are still the biggest sellers.

HOW SIGNIFICANT IS THE GRAPE VARIETY TO YOUR WINE-BUYING PUBLIC?

With regard to our regional market, the grape variety is not significant if we're talking in terms of the generally accepted global varieties such as Cabernet Sauvignon, Merlot, Pinot Noir, Chardonnay, Sauvignon Blanc, and Riesling. We have built a very solid regional business on the internationally *unknown* varieties: Concord, Catawba, Norton, Vignoles, Vidal, Traminette, Chambourcin, and a few lesser-known grapes.

I think too many people are overly focused on the "noble" European varieties. Many regions of the world have local, relatively unknown varieties that make incredible wines. The average person simply wants an enjoyable, affordable glass of wine and really doesn't care about the variety. They want an attractive package and an enjoyable taste, and they want the winery experience to be unpretentious and consumer-friendly. I always tell people to drink the wine you like, not the wine someone tells you to like.

I COULDN'T AGREE WITH YOU MORE. DID YOU KNOW THIS INSTINCTIVELY, OR DID IT COME THROUGH THE SCHOOL OF HARD KNOCKS?

Funny you should ask! Many years ago, when I was young and foolish, I suggested to my father that we eliminate Concord from our varietal mix since I thought it was beneath our dignity as serious winemakers. Dad said he'd think about it. The next year we needed a bit more to supply demand, the next year more. Boy, was I ever wrong. Five years ago I planted what one leading Concord researcher described as the most modern Concord vineyard he had ever seen. This humble variety is now our number one seller, because our customers really like it.

WHAT ADVICE WOULD YOU GIVE A NEW GROWER WHO'S JUST GETTING STARTED?

Don't get hung up on particular varieties. At our place, if someone says, "I like Merlot," my response is, "Why don't you try our Norton or Chambourcin?" Most find they like these alternative varieties—assuming, of course, the wines are of high quality. You must have good growers and winemakers if you are going to compete with the mainstream varieties. The most important component is price. There is an incredible array of high-quality wine in the lower price range on the market today, so your wines must be able to stand on their own against wine from anywhere.

In today's wine market, consumers love to visit retail tasting rooms, where they can sample a variety of wines to decide what they like before making their purchase.

CLASSIFYING GRAPES VARIETIES

For the vintner considering which grapes to plant, a good starting point is to break down available varieties into broad categories.

Vinifera: This is the family of grapes from which most classic European wines are made; the species originated in eastern Asia. Vinifera grapes thrive in warm moderate climates. Familiar names include: Cabernet Sauvignon, Chardonnay, Garnacha, Malbec, Pinot Noir, Riesling, Sauvignon Blanc, and Tempranillo.

Native North American Varieties: These hearty heirloom varieties grew wild in North America long before vinifera varieties were imported. They formed the basis for the early American wine industry in the eastern United States with well-known wineries such as Mogen David, Taylor, and Great Western. Many consider these varieties to be juice and jelly grapes because of their big forward fruity/grapy flavors. Familiar names are Catawba, Concord, Delaware, Dutchess, Niagara, Norton, and Scuppernong.

Hybrids: Hybrids are genetic crosses developed to combine the delicate flavor characteristics of classic vinifera varieties with heartier varieties that have adapted to local conditions; they are favored for extreme climates with greater humidity, more heat, and colder winter temperatures. Best known are French-American hybrids such as Chambourcin, Frontenac, Seyval Blanc, and Vidal Blanc.

WHEN I LEFT MY DAD'S VINEYARD IN 1980, I SWORE I WOULD NEVER GROW GRAPES AGAIN. TOO MANY SUMMERS BENT OVER HOEING WEEDS. MISERABLE MEMORIES OF ITCHY, WATERING EYES DURING PICKING SEASON. MY RESOLVE LASTED THROUGH THE NEXT FEW YEARS OF ESTABLISHING A NEW WINERY—SANS VINEYARD—WITH MY WIFE AND PARTNER LEE. IT LASTED THROUGH OUR FIRST EARLY SEASONS WHEN I WAS DETERMINED TO BUY ALL THE GRAPES WE NEEDED FROM HIGH-QUALITY GROWERS IN THE REGION. IT LASTED UNTIL OUR TWO YOUNGEST SONS ENTERED THE INEVITABLE TEENAGE HORMONAL STRUGGLE AND THE CALL OF THE MALL RESOUNDED LOUD AND CLEAR EVERY WEEKEND. AND THEN I HAD THIS BRILLIANT REVELATION: WHY NOT KEEP THEM BUSY FIFTEEN HOURS A DAY HOEING WEEDS IN THE VINEYARD?

CHAPTER 3:
PLANTING A VINEYARD

It's a common practice in newly planted vineyards to put planting tubes around the small vines to help direct upward growth, protect the trunk from predators, and separate the vines from weeds.

In the end, we got a couple of healthy strong young men who learned the value of hard work and what it means to earn their own money, and Lee and I got a beautiful well-tended vineyard. I can't help but believe that the preservation of many other great vineyards on this planet has occurred for similar reasons. Regardless of the reasons for establishing a vineyard, there's a lot to do before reaping the reward of your first harvest.

Some winegrowers do not use a trellis to support the weight of the crop and the year's green growth. In the case of these old Zinfandel vines ("bush trained") in Sonoma, California, the trunk of the vine is large enough to carry and stabilize the upper part of the vine.

PREPARING THE SITE AND THE SOIL PRIOR TO PLANTING

In the case of new vineyards on sites where vineyards have never been previously planted, pits are dug to observe subsoils where half the plant will live. Based on the results, it might be necessary to install some type of drainage underground to alleviate wet soils. There are weed-, tree-, and earth-moving considerations to eliminate competition, maintain topsoil, and control water runoff.

A few other considerations prior to planting: analyze the soil for nutrient content so adjustments can be made if necessary to achieve healthy soils, eliminate hardy weeds, address parasites by applying pesticides, and improve the organic matter of the soil by growing and plowing in Sudan grass or amendments.

LAYING OUT THE VINEYARD AND SETTING THE VINES

The layout of a vineyard is simply a map that shows where each vine and post will be located. Ideally, the layout will optimize sun and wind exposure but will also take into consideration water runoff. An additional consideration is space for headlands, where equipment can safely turn, and the grand finale harvest operation can be staged.

Meanwhile, the new grapevine plants that arrive dormant (so tender buds and green growth are not knocked off) are kept cool with wet roots until planting day.

Now, either a cut is made or a hole is dug or drilled before each vine is set into moist ground, with its roots spread and aimed down. Next, loose, moist soil is packed around the vine, and the grower pulls it upward to ensure downward root direction and depth of 10 to 15 inches (25 to 37 cm) below the vineyard floor level. If the vine is grafted, the graft union is set at 2 inches (5 cm) above the vineyard floor level and held there as soil is firmly tamped around the vine.

ROW SPACING AND VINE SPACING

There are two kinds of spacing that are important in a vineyard—the distance between the rows (alleys), and the distance between the vines in each row (vine spacing)—and both are significant in determining how many vines can be planted per acre (planting density). The guiding principles in establishing vineyard spacing are optimization of site and plant potential and convenient access to vines for spraying, harvesting, and other vineyard operations.

In the Old World, when planting was done by horse and plow and the tiniest parcel of land represented a family's greatest wealth, rows were narrow to intensify planting and increase yield per acre; it was not uncommon to find 3,000 vines per acre (0.4 ha) or spacing of 12 inches (30.5 cm) between vines with 3-foot (91 cm)-wide alleys. In more modern times, as large-scale vineyards became the norm in New World regions where land was cheap and practically virgin—and tractors were big enough to tow heavy mechanized equipment—vine spacing expanded as well. By the early 1970s, typical vine spacing had grown to 8 or 10 feet (2.4 to 3 m), with alleys of 15 feet (4.6 m) or more.

Today, smaller, less vigorous vines with less space between vines and rows have again become fashionable, partly because prime vineyard land has now become a limited resource in areas such as California's Napa Valley, and partly because today's well-educated viticulturists believe that vines do not need a great deal of space to produce moderate crops of top quality.

In winter a wild cover crop of mustard paints a bright splash of color down every row of this California vineyard, at the same time stabilizing the soil against erosion in spring. The cover crop can be plowed under for nutritional value.

BUILDING AND ESTABLISHING THE TRELLIS

The trellis is a support system for the vine designed to maximize quality and production by directing its growth upward or outward over a series of wires. It facilitates the various vineyard maintenance tasks that need to be done, such as pruning dead wood in winter; shaping, trimming, and spraying the vines during spring and summer; and harvesting the grapes in fall. The vintner's goal is for the trellis to support a canopy—the complete aboveground part of the plant—that is in perfect balance with the belowground root system.

A trellis consists of a series of horizontal wires attached to rows of vertical wood or metal posts, securely attached on both ends of the row by end posts deeply anchored in the ground. If irrigation is used in the vineyard, it is typically attached to one of the lower trellis wires. In a typical setup, a water emitter is installed on either side of the vines in the permanent irrigation lines attached to the first wire on the trellis. There are many different trellising styles, with distinct names such as Scott Henry, Geneva double curtain, and Hudson

In arid regions, watering the vines has become a high art form. In a typical setup, a water emitter is installed on either side of the vines in the permanent irrigation lines attached to the first wire on the trellis.

River umbrella. Some are low, some are high, some employ a single series of wires, and others have two sets of wires in a "Y" formation. Regardless of shape, what all trellises have in common is that they are designed to enhance some aspect of growing grapes, such as positioning the fruit for better sun exposure or developing more fruitful buds. In terms of the bottom line, the installation of the trellising system is one of the most costly single investments of establishing a vineyard.

At this point, when the critical decisions about site and grape varieties have been made, and when the new vines are planted and the trellis installed, a new vintner usually feels like a new homeowner who has just signed myriad papers necessary to complete the sale. You picked it, you own it, you've fallen in love with it (and probably broken the bank) … now you just have to move in and get on with the day-to-day tasks associated with ongoing yearly maintenance.

Undulating hillside plantings like this vineyard in Germany's Mosel Valley have to be painstakingly tailored to the lay of the land and planted by hand; flat sloping sites are more quickly and evenly planted by laser-sited planters.

Surveying the vineyards with Gary Pisoni is an adults-only roller-coaster ride. With the shotgun by his side, few birds make the mistake of stopping for a snack during harvest.

INTERVIEW WITH:
GARY PISONI, PISONI VINEYARDS & WINERY
SANTA LUCIA HIGHLANDS, CALIFORNIA, UNITED STATES

THE IMAGE OF GARY PISONI THAT STICKS IN MY MIND IS OF A WILD MAN IN A JEEP WITH A SILVER SHOTGUN, BARRELING UP A HILL AND FLYING OVER THE TOP, WHILE DRIVING A GROUP OF US THROUGH HIS PINOT NOIR VINEYARD.

A few minutes earlier, he had encouraged us to bring our glasses of wine along, and those of us who were stupid enough to listen to him were now in dire danger of losing both our wildly pricey glass of Pinot Noir and our cookies. (I think Gary has cleaned a lot of Pinot Noir off the seats of that jeep.) It was the ride of a lifetime, and it was worth it!

Gary Pisoni is a larger-than-life California winegrower with uncompromised practices in the vineyard; he produces fruit for premium California vintners and has gained much press and prestige for his Pisoni Estate Pinot Noir. His story is about vines and wines and family heritage: His parents started farming vegetables in the Salinas Valley in 1946. Gary started planting the Pisoni Vineyards in 1982, and today he works with his two sons, Mark and Jeffrey, who have taken the family farm to the next level by adding "& Winery" after "Pisoni Vineyards."

GARY, YOU ARE SUCH A HIGHLY REGARDED GRAPE GROWER. YOU HAVE ACHIEVED WHAT EVERY GRAPE GROWER DREAMS ABOUT. WHY ARE YOU SO SUCCESSFUL?

I just love grapes and I love wine.

HOW DID YOU GET INTO GROWING GRAPES?

My father had a large farm where we grew vegetables. But I fell in love with wine and started collecting wines in college, so after I graduated, I decided I wanted to plant wine grapes on the farm. We had this little ranch where we raised horses and cattle, and I was determined to plant a vineyard there. I started with a couple of acres, but eventually it grew to 50 or 60 acres (20 to 24 ha).

AND YOUR DAD DIDN'T RESIST YOU?

He resisted me a lot! After I told him I wanted to plant wine grapes, my father looked at me and said, "Gary, aren't you satisfied? We farm 1,000 acres (404.7 ha)—lettuce, celery, broccoli, asparagus, cauliflower. Why do you have to plant wine grapes up in those mountains?" And I said, "Dad, have you ever been invited to a black-tie lettuce tasting?" And then he kind of got it.

The most common type of vineyard trellis is called vertical shoot position (VSP). In this system, shoots are trained vertically between catch wires to become a thin layer of photosynthesizing leaves, while all the crop is set on a lower wire to expose the fruit to sun and air circulation.

"My father said, 'We farm 1,000 acres—lettuce, celery, broccoli, asparagus, cauliflower. Why do you have to plant wine grapes up in those mountains?' And I said, 'Dad, have you ever been invited to a black-tie lettuce tasting?'"

DID YOU STUDY VITICULTURE AT SCHOOL?

No, actually—I received my degree in psychology. That went over big with my dad, too. One day he said to me, "Gary, what the hell you gonna do with psychology?" And I said, "Talk to the grapes." But I've evolved since then. Now I listen to the grapes.

SO THAT'S YOUR SECRET TO PLANTING SUCCESSFUL VINEYARDS?

Yes, plus a little help from various sources. At first I had a friend teach me a little bit about planting grapes, back in 1982. And since then I've planted maybe twenty, twenty-five different vineyards, and got a little bit better on every one. I asked a lot of questions and I took some classes, and I read as many books as I could find about growing grapes. Eventually, I got really smart and sent my two sons to college to study it. And then we refined it a lot. Now, one kid makes the wine, and the other kid grows the grapes.

WHAT DO YOU LOVE MOST ABOUT PLANTING GRAPES?

The beautiful part about planting grapes is seeing them grow and taking care of them. We're farmers. We've been farmers all our lives. We love working with the earth. And the other thing that is really interesting is to see the different wines that result from our grapes and to see how the special things we do in the vineyard can affect them so much.

LIKE WHAT?

One thing we do is vertical shoot positioning so our shoots grow straight up. We have no lazy leaves. They all conduct photosynthesis, using sunlight to create sugar. You see, it's not really us who make the wine. Nature makes the wine and we're just the custodians who take care of things.

Here in the Santa Lucia Highlands, it's very important to have all of the vineyard row directions pointing north. A north-to-south row direction gets the best sun exposure. And then we make sure we have the right rootstock on the vines; the rootstock has to match the soils, which depends on whether you have shallow soils or deep soils. We rip the soils very deep, usually 4 to 5 feet (1.2 to 1.5 m) deep, because there's a hard pan underneath, and we want to break that so the roots can grow deep into the soil. If your roots can only go down a few feet, then your vines will suffer because they cannot reach enough water and nutrients, and the canopy—everything aboveground—will have limited growth as well.

PLEASE EXPLAIN THE PROCESS OF RIPPING THE SOILS.

You could just pull a furrow and drop the vines in. But no, we rip the soils, then we disc and chisel and we really work up the ground, and then we dig a hole by hand and put the vine in. It's really rough work digging all those holes by hand! At the same time, we put in stakes and the wires for the trellis. Actually, to start, we just install the first one to hold the irrigation lines; the rest of the wires we can put in later.

DO YOU NEED TO IRRIGATE IN YOUR AREA?

Definitely. We get an average of 10 to 13 inches (30.5 to 33 cm) of rain during the winter months, so we have to irrigate during the summer, about 3 to 4 gallons (11.4 to 15 L) per vine, about every fourteen to twenty-one days. That's another thing you want to think about right up front when you're establishing the vineyard, so you can get the irrigation set up right. You want to make sure you don't have any skips or any misses in the drip lines—it's so hard to come back the next few years and replant, because then you're irrigating the older grapes differently than the new young ones.

THAT'S A LOT OF WATER! DO YOU WORRY ABOUT ROOT ROT?

No, we have one emitter, where each plant is, about 12 to 18 inches (30.5 to 45.7 cm) on each side of the vine, and that makes the roots reach out farther, so you don't get any root rot. Also, we're very fortunate because our soils have really good drainage, so the water moves through quickly. It could rain hard today and you could go out there tomorrow and the water would be gone.

HOW DO YOU PLANT? DO YOU LASER PLANT?

No, we don't laser plant because our lands usually have a slope to them. You need to plant your vineyard to fit your land. If it's a steep slope, we put in terraces. That's a lot of work, but it's better to start out right and do everything right from the beginning, otherwise you've got forty years of problems to deal with later. After planting maybe twenty or twenty-five vineyards, I think we've finally figured it out.

In 1982 when I first planted, I didn't know what I was doing. I had to fake it. And then when people came from the University of California to talk to me about pruning and other techniques, I didn't really get it. But every time you plant a vineyard, you get it a little better than the last one. And finally, in the last few years, I became a vine. Now I understand it and how it really works.

YOU MENTIONED YOUR SLOPES AND TERRACES, AND I'D LIKE TO KNOW MORE ABOUT YOUR REGION, THE SANTA LUCIA HIGHLANDS.

We're in the foothills of the Santa Lucia Mountain Range, overlooking the Salinas River Valley, about 25 miles (40.2 km) southeast of Monterey Bay. We're in a nice location for cool-climate grapes, which is important because we grow mostly Pinot Noir and Chardonnay. We have the prevailing winds that come off the ocean every day to keep it cool, and we have the fog, which is also cooling.

"It's not really us who make the wine. Nature makes the wine and we're just the custodians who take care of things."

AND YOU'RE THE GUY WHO PUT IT ON THE MAP!

We're like a big team here. There are more than 5,000 acres (2,023 ha) currently under cultivation here, and more than ten wineries in the appellation. We're all innovators, running living laboratories. We all compare notes and ideas. We work together to grow the best wine possible. One thing I started early was to form long-term partnerships with the small wineries we sell to, some great properties such as Patz & Hall, Siduri, ROAR, Peter Michael, and Miura.

WHAT ABOUT THE FUTURE? ANY MORE VINEYARDS PLANNED?

No, I don't think so. I don't know for sure, but I think we're finally done planting vineyards. Anyway, the Highlands region is almost completely planted now.

WHAT WOULD YOU TELL SOMEONE WHO'S THINKING OF GETTING INTO THE BUSINESS ABOUT WHAT CAN GO WRONG?

A lot of things can go wrong. You might not rip the soil enough. Or you don't have your irrigation set up right, so you might not be able to water the vines fast enough and some might die. You might have the wrong rootstock. You might have the wrong bud wood—if you have Cabernet and you're in a Pinot Noir place. That's really important—you want to make sure you don't plant Zinfandel in a cool climate. You have to spray properly when the vines are young and during each growing season so you don't get mildew in the wood. Mildew never goes away.

It all comes down to the fact that you have to know your stuff and take it very seriously, because every time you make a mistake, it takes four years to fix it. To replant is a four-year goof up. My uncle used to always say, it's easy when you know how!

BUT SOMETIMES IT TAKES A LONG TIME TO LEARN HOW! WHAT WOULD YOU RECOMMEND IF SOMEONE CAME UP TO YOU AND WAS CONSIDERING PLANTING IN THE HIGHLANDS? WHAT WOULD BE THE BIG THINGS YOU'D RECOMMEND HE OR SHE DO?

The opposite of what I said about things that can go wrong! Have the right row direction. Rip the soil very well. Get the right clone and rootstock. Go to conferences. Get in touch with your local farm advisers and cooperative extension, because they understand the details of an area very well. Ask a lot of questions, and talk to your neighbors—if you're lucky enough to have some friendly neighbors.

Because uniformity makes vineyard maintenance easier, laser-activated planters such as this one at the Waltz Vineyard in Lancaster, Pennsylvania, have become popular for vineyard planting.

But here's my real advice. Love wine. If your heart's not in it and you don't drink wine, grape growing is not that much fun. You want to try to make the best wine possible, so it's something you're very proud of and something you enjoy sharing with your friends and family. It's a great life, and it's even better for me now that I share it with my boys. Every vintage we feel that we get a little closer to our goal of growing the best grapes possible and producing the kind of wines that represent our vineyard and the dedication of our family.

TRELLISING SYSTEMS

GENEVA DOUBLE CURTAIN
The Geneva double curtain trellising system with its two parallel canopies was developed at New York State's Cornell University to increase the capacity of a vine for both green growth and crop. Some vines can carry twice as much crop this way.

SCOTT HENRY
The very tall Scott Henry trellis consists of two vertical canopies, or "curtains," one directly above the other. This system increases the vine's capacity by almost twice the crop.

HIGH WIRE SPRAWL
In a high wire sprawl the vine's trunk is trained to a high wire and shoots are allowed to droop down to the ground. The fruit is typically shaded by the green growth; the advantage is that this system requires low maintenance.

This track-mounted post pounder at the Waltz Vineyard in Lancaster, Pennsylvania, is inserting an end post at an angle so the anchor can be installed below it. End posts anchor the trellis wires.

A common sight in the vineyard during late spring! This cluster of flowers is hermaphroditic (self-pollinating) and will later become a cluster of grapes.

ONGOING CULTURAL PRACTICES—THE DAY-TO-DAY WORK WE DO IN THE VINEYARD—ARE A TRUE CONVERGENCE OF NATURE AND NURTURE. ON ONE HAND, WE ARE FARMING A SITE AND SOILS THAT MOTHER NATURE PROVIDED AND DEALING WITH THE WEATHER SHE THROWS OUR WAY EACH DAY. ON THE OTHER HAND, THERE ARE MANY THINGS WE CAN DO TO CHANGE AND ENHANCE LIFE AROUND THE VINEYARD TO HELP US MEET OUR GOALS OF GROWING EXCELLENT GRAPES (FOR THIS VINTAGE) AND STRONG VINES (SO THERE IS A NEXT VINTAGE).

CHAPTER 4:
VINEYARD CULTURE: A YEAR ON THE LAND

I think of a grapevine as having the same temperament as my son Bayen when he was two years old. He was either on or off: busy, busy, busy building things, taking things apart, generally requiring attention … or totally zonked out asleep. When a vine is out there in the warm sun it's continuously pushing growth, moving things around its system, and doing everything it can to produce progeny. Then, in winter, nutrients retreat to the roots and the vine goes to sleep (dormant).

In the vineyard, there are maintenance jobs to do when the subject is finally sleeping, and a heck of a lot to do when it's awake and growing.

WINTER VINEYARD MAINTENANCE

PRUNING

The winegrower's biggest winter job is pruning the grape vines, although some people start pruning in late fall, after harvest, when leaves have dropped and wood quality can be evaluated. This first pass through the vineyard is an opportunity to shape the plant onto the trellis, cut off dead wood, and remove excess growth from the previous year. After a healthy growing season, a mature vine can have hundreds of potentially fruitful buds, most of which are found on ripe brown canes (matured green shoots from the previous growing season)—far more than desired—so pruning serves as a way of setting the year's crop level by determining how many buds to leave on each plant.

The potential crop load, the number of buds left on the vine, and the location of fruitful buds are determined by each variety's fruitfulness and the vine's condition after the previous harvest season and the current winter. Vines that are spaced far apart are left with more buds in order to fill the trellis with green growth and might have 100 or more buds; closely spaced, extremely arid or old vineyards may have as few as one fruitful bud.

Any pruning shears used to prune rose bushes will work just fine on a grape vine (although my own favorite is Felco, adapted from aluminum sheet cutters). There are also electric and pneumatic shears.

Mechanical pruning is faster but not as accurate as hand pruning because it leaves no decision making for individual vines. These large tractor-mounted machines are arrangements of blades and optical devices capable of trimming multiple rows at a time. Although mechanical pruning involves a much larger capital outlay to purchase the equipment it is becoming more common because of its time-saving advantage, and simply requires more re-finements later in the season. For example, if too many canes or buds are left on the vine, a rotating brush is used later to sweep off excess buds or shoots when they are young and tender and before they sap too much energy from the vine.

EQUIPMENT REPAIR AND MAINTENANCE

Winter downtime is also the preferred time for vineyard and equipment repair and maintenance, such as replacing worn tractor tires, splicing broken trellis wires, replacing broken posts, filling potholes, and so on.

Like most gardens, vineyards face a never-ending battle with weeds. On terraced sites, steep slopes, and tight spaces, they are often hunted down and grubbed out by those stout of back with a hoe strong enough to resist the stony soil.

PRUNING

Before pruning: Once leaves have fallen and winter sets in, the vine's wood hardens and ripens to a brown or gray color. These Barbera vines await their winter "haircut" from the winegrower's pruning shears.

After pruning: When healthy ripe wood and buds are identified, vines are pruned to slightly more than their ideal crop potential. As the season progresses, shoots and clusters are removed to fine-tune the crop.

Weather and pests can be devastating to grapevines. These injured trunks and canes were pruned out during the winter and are piled for burning later.

These Pinot Noir vines have been "spur pruned." In this system, the previous growing season's canes are cut back to short spurs for a balance of green growth and crop the following year.

Head-pruned vines can be freestanding and cultivated from four directions because there are no trellis wires. In this system, the fruit is shaded and canes grow downward.

SPRING AND SUMMER VINEYARD WORK

TRAIN VINES TO THE TRELLIS
This secures the vine so it stays safely away from equipment traveling down the rows, spreads the canopy to allow sun and air movement, creates manageable, uniform fruit zones, and allows spray penetration.

MOW OR CULTIVATE ALLEYS BETWEEN ROWS
This helps control moisture, air movement, and nutritional competition.

CULTIVATE, BURN, OR CHEMICALLY CONTROL WEEDS UNDER THE TRELLIS
Although a controlled population of certain weeds is encouraged in organic vineyards, they typically make the vineyard look un-tended, compete for water and nutrients, and create habitats for pests and mildews.

OBSERVE AND ANALYZE
The winegrower uses a combination of visual observation and soil and tissue analysis to understand the health of each vineyard block and variety over the course of each growing season.

APPLY FERTILIZER OR BENEFICIAL ORGANISMS TO SOIL OR LEAVES
It's routine in a healthy vineyard to test for and add nutrients and trace minerals (amendments), but the vine will also benefit (and be better balanced) from a healthy underground population of micro-organisms, commonly found in compost.

MONITOR SOIL MOISTURE AND IRRIGATE IF NECESSARY
It is true that grapevines like dry feet, but in arid regions moisture must be added to sustain beneficial organisms, cool the plant, and serve as a medium to carry trace minerals and nutrients.

APPLY FUNGICIDES AND PESTICIDES (SPRAYING)
Grapevines look delicious to insects, molds, and diseases. Weak vines and humid climates fight a larger array of pests, but all winegrowers share concerns for the likes of powdery mildew, black rot, and Japanese beetles.

REMOVE CROWDED SHOOTS (SHOOT THINNING)
Excess shoots carry excess crop, shade the fruit, and inhibit air movement and spray coverage.

REMOVE LEAVES IN FRUIT ZONE (LEAFING)
Once leaves near the grape clusters have provided nutrients, assuring a good flower set, many are removed. Unshaded or sun-dappled clusters are known to develop higher sugars and desirable flavors.

BAD BUGS AND GOOD BUGS

In centuries past, winegrowers depended on the sensitivity of rose bushes to forewarn of mildew and insect infestations headed their way. Today, a more sophisticated understanding of predator life cycles allows earlier intervention ... but the rose bush remains a beautiful tradition at the Historic Hopewell Vineyard in southeast Pennsylvania.

Compost is becoming a more common soil amendment as today's vignerons discover the value of diverse biological activity in the soil.

SPRAYING

Small vineyard sprayers are often towed by a tractor as they distribute pesticides or foliar fertilizer over the vines.

In larger, more mechanized vineyards, huge, over-the-row sprayers accomplish the same thing in a lot less time! These behemoth machines can do other vineyard jobs as well, including mechanical pruning, hedging, and harvesting.

At his famous biodynamic vineyard, Coulée de Serrant in Savennières, France, Nicolas Joly cultivates according to the theories of Rudolf Steiner whereby organic preparations replace conventional sprays and fertilizers, and seasonal activities are performed according to Earth and its relation to the cosmos.

TUCK SHOOTS INTO TRELLIS (POSITIONING)

Long leafy vine shoots produce better quality buds for next year when they grow upright, supported by the trellis, in their assigned zone. Tucking also helps them stay out of the way of vineyard operations.

REMOVE EXCESS CROP (CLUSTER THINNING, OR GREEN HARVESTING)

A vine carrying too large a crop may dilute fruit concentration and cause imbalances in traits such as acidity because the plant has to work too hard to distribute its precious resources. Although it seems economically advantageous to bring in a large crop, the result of less flavorful grapes is deficient juice and less interesting wines, often requiring costly manipulation in the cellar. Overcropping can also damage and weaken vines, which affects their future contribution to the vineyard.

REMOVE EXCESSIVELY LONG SHOOTS (HEDGING)

Shoots that sprawl upward and pass the top trellis wire can infringe on neighboring vines and create an umbrella effect that shades the fruit, creating inconsistencies in operations and fruit quality. Hedging can occur as early as mid-spring and also be required later, within a few weeks of harvest.

TODAY VERSUS TOMORROW

Most of these routine cultural practices and vineyard maintenance operations are focused on one goal: bringing in the crop. Foremost in the vintner's mind throughout the season are questions such as, "How many grapes will we pick this year?" and "What's going to happen to the crop if these rains continue?"

A secondary concern is always playing in the background as well, reminding the vintner that the end of this season is the beginning of the next. Although today's focus is the progeny of the vine, tomorrow's will be healthy canes and buds for the future. It is a delicate game of give and take as the winegrower lives both for this year and next, belowground and above. There is the joy of creating an unbridled success, tempered by weather letdowns, predator problems, and other complications that contribute to the complex unrepeatable "recipe" that is the vintage.

ANATOMY OF A GRAPE VINE

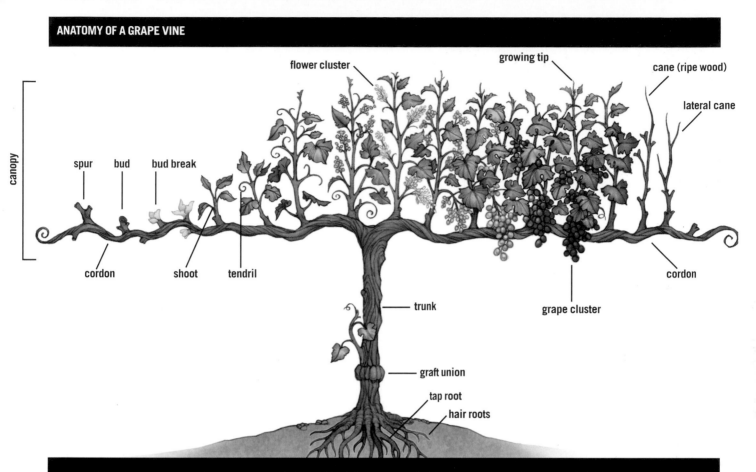

canopy

flower cluster

growing tip

cane (ripe wood)

lateral cane

spur

bud

bud break

cordon

shoot

tendril

trunk

grape cluster

cordon

graft union

tap root

hair roots

FEEDING IN THE VINEYARD

Vineyard predators come in a variety of shapes, sizes, and taste in vine, from woodchucks to deer, insects to birds. Between them all, they will eat just about any part of the vine. One of the most terrifying predators is a migrating flock of birds that drop in for a quick snack of a ton or two of grapes on their way south for their winter vacation. Large mammals such as deer can almost fly over an electric fence and always seem to prefer their grapes about a week less ripe than a vintner does. The results of a visit by a deer family of three will break your heart: a methodical stripping of grape clusters, at the rate of about 150 pounds (68 kg) a night.

Bird netting, often applied over the vines to keep out pests when the fruit has ripened, has to be removed in order to pick the grapes.

THE FOUR SEASONS IN A VINEYARD

Early spring: Buds first "break" when soil temperatures exceed 50°F and nutrients stored from the previous growing season fuel initial growth.

Late spring: Mature vines push tender green shoots and begin to fill the length of the trellis during "the great period of growth."

Autumn: As the sun becomes lower in the sky, days are shorter, nights are cooler, green shoots mature to become ripe brown canes, older leaves stop functioning and turn color, and the long-awaited fruit is picked.

Vineyards are not all about work! Nothing is more enticing than a picnic in the vineyard or a mad dash between neat rows of vines on a summer day.

Summer: Over the summer, the vine's canopy fills, clusters flower and become berries, fruit begins to color, and the vine shifts its focus from just getting big to storing nutrients for its progeny, the grapes.

Winter: A good winegrower has grown high-quality grapes for this vintage; a great winegrower has also made sure the vine has stored sufficient nutrients for a long winter's nap and energetic kickoff next spring.

Aljoscha Goldschmidt is one of the
new breed of Italian winemakers
energized by new possibilities and
technology, with feet planted firmly in
the depth and understanding of
tradition.

INTERVIEW WITH:
ALJOSCHA GOLDSCHMIDT
CORZANO E PATERNO, SAN CASCIANO, TUSCANY, ITALY

AS MY FIRST SANGIOVESE VINEYARD WAS MATURING IT OCCURRED TO ME THAT I HAD NO DEPTH OF UNDERSTANDING FOR THIS EXTRAORDINARY GRAPE. SO I CREATED A LIST OF HIGHLY RESPECTED OLD WORLD, NEW AND INNOVATIVE, LARGE AND SMALL PRODUCERS IN TUSCANY AND ASKED THEM IF I COULD INTERVIEW THEM ABOUT SANGIOVESE.

With a week's worth of visits scheduled, Lee and I flew to Italy and had the education of a lifetime as we went from vineyards to cellars and tables. It was like nothing we had experienced before. As it turned out, the most dynamic and delicious place we visited was Corzano e Paterno in Chianti. There we were greeted like family, were taken through the vineyards, became enamored by a tiny centuries-old cellar, and tasted wines with winemaker Aljoscha Goldschmidt.

Aljoscha is a very serious winegrower with the passion of a great artist who appreciates the raw unpredictable power of any given season and has seen enough of them to show his flexibility and skill. He has been a part of Corzano e Paterno since 1973, when he began working there with his uncle and family at the ripe old age of twelve. Today, it is still very much a family *fattoria*—farm—and Aljoscha is farm director, general manager, and winemaker. It was a pleasure to catch up with him again recently during one of his whirlwind promotional tours.

This painfully beautiful scene of the Corzano e Paterno vineyards and fields, where cattle graze to supply the family's small creamery, is not uncommon in the Chianti district of Italy.

"Growing wine is a fascinating, endless learning process. It's not all about knowing facts or listening to the weather forecast. It's also about using your instincts. Sometimes you do things for no other reason than how you feel."

I HAVE SUCH GREAT MEMORIES OF TRAVELING THROUGH THE UNDULATING HILLS OF TUSCANY, INTOXICATED BY THE GORGEOUS LANDSCAPE OF OLIVE AND CYPRESS TREES AND VINEYARDS, AND ARRIVING AT THE GATES OF CORZANO E PATERNO. THE WHOLE FARM WAS SO ENCHANTING AND TIMELESS. HOW DID THIS ALL COME TO BE?

My Uncle Wendel Gelpke was a Swiss architect who bought the original Corzano farm in 1973. He, his son Tillo, and I planted 6 hectares (14.8 acres) originally, and then in 1975 he acquired the adjoining La Fattoria de Paterno, and we planted more vines on the Corzano hill. You could say I grew up at Corzano e Paterno—I've been doing this since I was twelve. Today we have 18 hectares (44.5 acres) of grapes, graze sheep, make cheeses, and are an *agriturismo* (agritourism) destination.

HOW HAS YOUR BUSINESS GROWN AND CHANGED OVER THE YEARS?

My uncle believed in self-sufficiency. Our goal has always been to create the finest end products from the raw materials at our disposal. Our cheeses are served at some of the finest restaurants in Europe and our wines have won international praise, so obviously we are very proud of all that we have accomplished as a family. Then in the 1980s the Chianti area embraced the agriturismo initiative to help the local farmers save the neglected buildings on their properties, so today we also have two renovated farmhouses and various apartments that we rent to visitors.

WHAT ARE YOUR VINEYARDS LIKE?

The soil is marine sediment, with a stratification of clay and limestone. Our altitude is 250 to 300 meters (820 to 984 feet). Slopes face south/southwest with a little east exposure. We mostly grow Sangiovese and have some Canailo, which is traditionally blended with Sangiovese for Chianti. A bit of Cabernet, which is very interesting, and a bit of Merlot, but it's not very interesting here because it ripens too early. We get too high alcohols and phenolics (bitterness) and it ripens too quickly. For whites we have Trebbiano, Malvesia (used for Vin Santo), Chardonnay, Sémillon, Sauvignon Blanc, and Petite Marseng.

As for climate, it's very dry here in May, June, and July, and very hot in August. We have rain in the autumn, and winter can be quite cold, often going to freezing. Our clay soils hold water, which is very important at the end of the Tuscan summer, when it's very hot and dry.

DESCRIBE YOUR VINEYARD ACTIVITIES BETWEEN DORMANCY AND HARVEST TIME.

We start with pruning, using mostly Guyot training—and then we tie the vines before growing starts. Buds come out and the growing seasons starts in April, so there is a great deal of pressure to get the pruning done on time. Two weeks after the buds come out the shoots are already 10 centimeters (4 inches) long, so we break off ones we don't want. You just can't keep everything growing!

After removing shoots, we wind the remaining ones into the wires so they grow up in a vertical way [rather than lean on the next plant]. By June, the flowering has happened and shoots are about at the top wire. The small green berries are set and we trim off the top of the shoots. If they get too long they fall down and hang over the rest of the vine and shade the grapes. Biodynamic growers recommend not lopping off these shoots, but I feel—like they do in Bordeaux—that we must have order.

By the end of June, the grape clusters are growing, gaining weight, and hanging down. Then we remove a few leaves, to allow some sunlight to hit the grapes, but not so much that they are exposed fully to our hot July and August sun. This is a lot of handwork but is helpful later at the green harvest in July and August, so you can see the clusters.

CAN YOU EXPLAIN "GREEN HARVEST"?

When the clusters are beginning to change color, we remove some from the vine. Which ones you remove vary from plant to plant and according to what your goals are. For instance, if there are two clusters, you remove the upper one because it's usually the less developed. If two clusters are touching, you remove one so it hangs free and has air moving around it. For a simple, everyday, light fruity red wine it's okay to leave some "second bunches," but for a more concentrated wine, you would keep the loose clusters and remove the densely packed bunches. For us, six clusters per vine is ideal, that's the equivalent of 1 kilogram (2.2 pounds). A kilo provides one bottle of wine.

Green harvest is usually our last handwork before picking. If it looks like it's going to be a late harvest, with risk of rot, we might take some leaves away to allow more sun and air to flow through. But we would only do that if the season is cool and harvest is expected to be in late October. It would be very dangerous to do that earlier when you have a hot strong sun and want the fruit protected.

ARE THERE ONE OR TWO KEY THINGS YOU DO IN THE VINEYARD TO MAKE GREAT WINE?

Growing wine is a fascinating, endless learning process. It's not all about knowing facts or listening to the weather forecast. It's also about using your instincts. Sometimes you do things for no other reason than how you feel. It might rain. It might be a hot, dry summer. The weather follows no rules, so sometimes you just have to do something because you feel like you understand Nature.

Another critical thing for me is the green harvest. The amount of grapes a plant carries tips the scale of dilution or concentration.

Corzano e Paterno is an agritourism-designated estate where guests spend their nights comfortably among the vineyards, grazing cattle, wine cellars, olive groves, and creamery.

ARE THERE CULTURAL PRACTICES INHERENT IN A TRADITIONAL REGION SUCH AS CHIANTI THAT INHIBIT YOUR CREATIVITY... OR FROM WHICH YOU BENEFIT?

It helps to be an internationally known region. We are building upon thousands of years of history, so we must be careful integrating new ways. In Chianti, we have rules—I believe we need certain rules—but the rules aren't excessive. We must use about 80 percent Sangiovese, but then we can add many other varieties. The list includes international varieties such as Syrah, Cabernet, Merlot; the official name for them is "complementary varieties." I don't like this—Chianti is made from indigenous varieties (only Saniovese and Canaiolo)—why add others just to be able to say you have international varieties? It's not Chianti if it tastes like somewhere else!

AFTER ALL THIS TIME, WHAT SUSTAINS YOUR PASSION FOR GROWING GRAPES?

Grapes give you the opportunity to make wine. It's a very noble way to do agriculture. It's sophisticated and magical. It makes me conscious of my surroundings, and the work is fascinating. Of course, there must be money, but the work is healthy, so for my family, it is not about money. It's about quality of life. My work is producing wine. My wife makes the cheese. We like our work. If you live in a beautiful place and have good wine and food, it's simply the best thing in the world.

HARVEST TIME IS WHEN I BECOME NICE AGAIN. THE LAST TWO OR THREE WEEKS OF THE GRAPE-GROWING SEASON, IN THE FINAL WEEKS BEFORE PICKING BEGINS, MY SKIN DOESN'T FIT, MY TEMPLES THROB, I LOSE CONFIDENCE IN EQUIPMENT REPAIRS, MY NEGOTIATIONS WITH THE WEATHERMAN GUARANTEEING CLEAR, DRY WEATHER FOR THE NEXT FEW WEEKS HAVE AGAIN FAILED, AND THERE ARE A LOT OF TEARS. I BEGIN TO FEEL LIKE AN OVERDUE PREGNANT WOMAN, PACING, WAITING, WONDERING WHEN IT'S ALL GOING TO BEGIN SO I CAN FINALLY COME FACE TO FACE WITH THE STRANGER I'VE BEEN GESTATING FOR NINE LONG MONTHS.

CHAPTER 5:
IT'S HARVEST TIME!

Hand picking is slow but gentle, leaving the berries intact until they hit the processing deck.

Harvest time is the one chance each year I have to use what I've learned over the past five, ten, thirty-nine years.

The hardest part of the harvest is pulling the trigger, making the final decision for when the first grapes will begin to roll in. Up to that moment, even if I've done everything right and the weather has been co-operative, I have probably imagined seven different scenarios about how it *might* go and the air crackles with anticipation.

When grapes begin to color (called veraison) the winegrower gets a strong indication of how much crop the vines can carry. If every cluster is evenly colored, the crop is about right. Those clusters that lag behind in color are typically dropped on the ground for a more uniform quality level.

EVALUATING THE GRAPES

As harvest approaches—around September/October in the Northern Hemisphere and February/March in the Southern Hemisphere—the vine is responding to the angle of the sun, the length of the day's light, and the late-season hormonal rush to make ripe berries. The vine's green growth has stopped and all of its energy is now focused on the fruit. For the vintner, these last few weeks before picking begins are a time of sampling the grapes, evaluating their condition, correcting any problems, and estimating their arrival on the crush pad. The biggest need at this critical time of year is knowledge, so we spend a great deal of time evaluating the fruit. This can be done in several ways.

SAMPLING IN THE VINEYARD

Every winemaker seems to have his or her own methods for sampling, but they all involve pulling representative samples from each block of each variety in each vineyard. These are tasted and visually evaluated for sugar, acid, tannins, appropriate flavors, ripeness of seeds, and condition of fruit. They are looking for consistent color, ripe flavors without herbaceousness or bitterness, and zero rot. Despite all the modern equipment and lab technology available, many still believe that final picking decisions are best left to the mouth of the winemaker.

ANALYSIS IN THE LAB

It would be impossible to identify each region and each winemaker's target numbers, but we can generalize. In the lab, a still winemaker (one not making Champagnes or sparkling wines) is typically looking for white grapes in the range of 3.2 to 3.4 pH (measurement of acidity) and 20° to 25° Brix (measurement of sugar content), and reds around 3.3 to 3.6 pH with 22° to 26° Brix.

If the numbers are right, a picking schedule might be launched; if not, the wait continues!

LAST CHANCE FOR CORRECTIONS

At this point in the game, if the vintner is not chasing four-footed predators out of the vineyard, laying out bird netting to protect the crop, or inviting hawks over for blackbird pie, there's not a lot left to do, or that can be done. But occasionally last-minute adjustments are made, especially by removing some of the hanging clusters (also called green harvesting; see "Interview with Aljoscha Goldschmidt" in chapter 4), if required by certain conditions:

■ If clusters are unevenly colored, drop those clusters. Unevenly colored clusters (exception: Pinot Grigio) indicate not only color deficiency, but also unripe seeds and underdeveloped flavors, which will affect the quality of the wine.
■ If predators have broken berry skins with their beaks or stingers immediately before harvest, there is a likelihood that the exposed juice is oxidized and has been infected with unknown yeast or bacteria. To allow that fruit in the cellar would be to give up control of fermentation, so drop those clusters.
■ If the vine is overcropped and struggling, desired color, smells, and flavors and the chemical balance will be diluted or compromised, so drop some clusters at least four weeks before harvest (while the vine still has time to ripen the remaining crop).
■ Mold and mildew on the berries will affect color and flavor of the finished wine, so these clusters should be removed before picking. One exception to this rule is when the *Botrytis cinerea* fungus (often called botrytis bunch rot or "noble rot") attacks the clusters, adding its own honeylike flavor and concentrating the sugars. *B. cinerea* can result in distinctive sweet dessert wines such as Sauternes and Tokaj.

PREPARING EQUIPMENT

Now that harvest is imminent in the vineyard, the winery crush pad or processing deck also needs to be readied for the soon-to-be-arriving grapes. Since processing equipment is used only once a year, no matter where or how it's been stored, it needs to be cleaned, test-operated, and thoroughly examined before grapes arrive. No matter how many years pass, no one will ever be able to explain how all those paper-thin dried-out grape skins magically appear on every piece of equipment after they were cleaned at the end of the previous season!

PICKING GRAPES

So we walk the rows, run the tests, ready the equipment, and then one day it finally happens. The taste and numbers are right, the plan moves into action, and the annual grape harvest begins!

The harvest may look bucolic and simple in pictures and movies but the logistics behind a real harvesting operation are complicated and businesslike. Days or weeks before the anticipated harvest date, picking lugs and bins will be brought out of storage and washed. On the actual day of picking, the small lugs will be stacked at the end of each vineyard row so that handpickers are never left idle and grapes are delivered to the crush pad as soon as possible while cool and fresh. For mechanical harvesting, whoever is overseeing the operation will have a good idea of the how much is expected to be harvested from the field being picked, and should have the right number of large bins, usually with one-ton capacity, readily available. Such containers, along with forklifts, trucks, and trailers, are either at the vineyard or going back and forth in an endless cycle of loading and unloading.

Because everything takes place out in the field, drinking water, meals, and first-aid supplies also have to be purchased, lined up, and imported to the vineyard site. And a "triage" system needs to be set up if multiple fields or vineyards reach optimum maturity and need to be picked and brought to the crush pad at the same time.

Hand picking requires large crews that have to be assembled in advance, because every other vintner in the area needs available labor at the same time. The time it takes to pick a particular field or vineyard depends on crop load and the number of available pickers. In small, family operations, the "crew" is usually made up of

the owners and any available friends and relatives; larger vineyards and wineries often have some permanent vineyard workers and access to migrant labor during the harvest period.

Baskets or buckets used for hand picking usually have a capacity of 15 to 50 pounds (6.8 to 22.7 kg). When filled, they are dumped into a nearby (larger) bin or trailer. Typically, empty baskets are set ahead of pickers so they don't have to stop when their basket is full. Because most grapes are picked and paid for by the basket or pound, this system accommodates everyone's needs.

A mechanical harvester is an expensive investment that comes into use just once a year. For those winegrowers who delay harvest for quality reasons, its speed of picking allows the grapes to hang until the last possible minute.

PREHARVEST CHECKLIST

Recalibrate the scale (to weigh the arriving grape bins).

Clean the big "must lines"—hoses and conveyors used for transferring crushed grapes.

Wash and test-run the (receiving) hopper, stemmer-crusher, and must pump.

Check mechanics, pressure gauges, and internal "bladder" on the press (this is the collapsible balloon inside the press that is inflated with air pressure to squeeze the juice away from the skins).

This one-ton bulk bin of Pinot Noir grapes will yield about 170 gallons (643.5 L) of juice, or three barrels of wine, equivalent to 850 bottles.

Even after careful picking, many wineries hand sort each cluster. Some wineries—wanting to assure the absolute best fruit—take it a step further and sort each berry of the cluster.

Assuming optimum conditions and stopping only for a meal and water breaks, the fastest pickers range between one and two tons of grapes a day. Depending on the trellising system and crop size, it takes one to four people to pick an acre (0.4 ha) in a day.

Hand picking is much slower than mechanical harvesting, but much gentler to the grapes, leaving the clusters intact until they hit the processing deck. The grapes are picked using hooked knives, picking shears, or some mighty tough hands. Some vintners may try to do a final field sorting at the same time, but this is difficult if the picking staff is motivated to fill the basket as quickly as possible.

Machine harvesting entails a sophisticated behemoth of a machine that straddles the vine and removes the grape clusters. No two harvesters are exactly alike, but the principle they work on is sudden violent motion, which shakes the vine and detaches the stem from the vine or the grapes from the cluster, leaving the berries as intact as possible. Because a high percentage of berries are broken in the process, great care is taken to move through the fields quickly—maybe with the grapes under a blanket of CO_2 to protect them from oxidation.

The prerequisites to achieve this goal include having a good supply of bins of the right size and capacity, lights if the harvesting is done at night, and a large level space where the bins can be safely organized and loaded. In addition to a skilled machine operator, backup help is needed to arrange the logistics of moving or hauling the full bins to the crush-pad site.

The goal of every vintner is to cut the clusters from the vines as quickly as possible, but it's also about not allowing "material other than grapes"—MOG—in with the grapes. It's amazing how many birds' nests, rocks, pieces of the trellis, T-shirts, and picking shears show up in the bins and then eventually find their way to the winery crush pad!

REACHING THE END

Harvest lasts as long as there are grapes to be picked. The number of days will depend on how many varieties (and what type) are planted, how many vineyards or acres are being picked, the amount of manpower available, and the particulars of a growing season, typically ranging from thirty to forty-five days. But a vineyard with early season varieties such as Vignoles as well as late-ripening varieties such as Barbera might be picking sporadically for sixty days! In a cool, minimal-sun season, harvest might be delayed for ten days and suddenly ended by an early frost, when leaves fall and no longer help ripen the grapes. Conversely, a hot, sunny vintage might hasten ripening, and therefore harvest, by several days. Whatever the length of the *vendange* (grape harvest), it is cause for great celebration when the last grapes are finally picked!

Eileen Crane, founding winemaker and C.E.O. at Domaine Carneros in California, enjoys a glass of bubbly on a beautiful patio overlooking the estate vineyard.

INTERVIEW WITH:
EILEEN CRANE
DOMAINE CARNEROS, NAPA, CALIFORNIA, UNITED STATES

WITH HER LEGENDARY WORK ETHIC, BRILLIANT PALATE, AND CLEAR VISION, EILEEN COULD HAVE DONE JUST ABOUT ANYTHING, BUT HER HEART WAS IN SPARKLING WINE.

I first met Eileen Crane when I was twenty-one and my favorite place to hang out was at the Culinary Institute of America (CIA), where she happened to be taking a wine class. I was winemaker by default at my father's Hudson Valley winery after he had suddenly gone from artist to media idol of the nascent premium eastern U.S. wine industry. Having just ingested the University of California's tome *The Technology of Winemaking*, I was convinced that the way to fully grasp winemaking was to move to California and study at UC Davis with other energized enology students and the masters of wine who were teaching there. That's about all I needed to tell Eileen, and she took it from there.

After moving from Connecticut to California and working her way up through the ranks of two prestigious sparkling wine facilities, she joined up with the French Champagne House of Taittinger and took the helm at their new California property in the Carneros region of Napa Valley. Over the past two decades, serving as both president and winemaker of Domaine Carneros, Eileen has steered this elegant winery straight into the forefront of the American sparkling wine industry.

Although the architecture of the elegant Domaine Carneros château is clearly influenced by its prestigious French connection to Champagne Taittinger, the wines are 100 percent California.

HOW DID YOU END UP IN YOUR FIRST WINEMAKING CLASS?

I had a master's degree in nutrition and was teaching at the University of Connecticut, and the Culinary Institute of America happened to be nearby. I was hearing a lot of buzz about the CIA, and decided to sign up for this ten-week course, even though I really had no background in cooking whatsoever.

It ended up being a lot of fun, but I have never worked so hard in my life! Despite fourteen-hour shifts, a few friends and I somehow found the time to take a wine class—and one night you came in and spoke to our club about winemaking. You also mentioned that there was this hot new winemaking program at UC Davis in California, and after the class I came up to you and asked for more information.

I called the university to make an appointment to talk with someone. When I finally met up with a professor at Davis, he said I would have to come and do four more years of undergraduate work, and then two more years on a master's degree. "I think you're wasting your time," he said. "Why don't you just get a Ph.D. in nutrition?"

And I said, "I'm going to be a winemaker." And he said, "I don't think so."

TALK ABOUT A CHALLENGE!

Yes, but he referred me to a new professor, Ann Noble, and she said, "Eileen, you don't need another degree. You've already got a master's in a science, so why don't you just come and take some classes and convince somebody you can do it." So I took two classes for two quarters and audited a bunch of other ones.

THAT WAS IN THE LATE 1970S AND IT MUST HAVE BEEN A VERY INTERESTING TIME TO BE AT DAVIS.

It was the spring of 1978 and a huge boom time for California wine. A whole array of interesting characters was there, including Randall Grahm (Bonny Doon) and Bo Barrett from Château Montelena. And Gil Nickel (who started Far Niente) and Bruce Cakebread (Cakebread Cellars) and Carol Anderson (S. Anderson Vineyard).

SO YOU ONLY STUDIED THERE FOR TWO QUARTERS?

Yes, and then I had to get a job! I was hired by Chandon (the California house of Moët & Chandon in Champagne) for a part-time tasting room position and almost starved that summer! But after six weeks I moved to the position of assistant pastry chef … and then a few weeks later their winemaker quit and they asked me if I was interested in helping out for the harvest period. I took the job, and then at the end of harvest, I became the full-time enologist, doing all the lab work. I was at Chandon for six years, and then I was hired by the Ferrer family of Spain (who own Freixenet) to work at the new sparkling wine facility they were building in California (Gloria Ferrer Winery).

WHAT WAS YOUR POSITION THERE?

When the company's Spanish representative offered me the job I asked who was going to be responsible for building the winery. He said, "Well, you are!" Then he went home to Spain and I knew basically nothing about construction and that was very scary. We started construction about a month after harvest, and in the meantime I had to find grapes and I had to find a production facility to press them. It was the hardest two years of my life. It was also the most exciting two years. (By the way, the project finished on time.)

"The numbers give you signals, the lab will tell you whether harvest is on the radar screen or not, but my final picking decisions are based on taste."

The best thing was it led to my current position at Domaine Carneros. At the end of our construction at Gloria Ferrer I was approached by the Taittinger family of Champagne Taittinger, who was planning to build a new California winery, about the same size, nearby.

I'D SAY IT WAS A GOOD MATCH SINCE YOU'VE BEEN THERE FOR WELL OVER TWENTY YEARS NOW! WHAT'S IT LIKE HAVING A FRENCH OWNER? WHO DECIDES HOW TO MAKE THE WINES—YOU OR (PRESIDENT) PIERRE-EMMANUEL TAITTINGER?

Taittinger has always taken a different approach than other French Champagne houses with California wineries. From the beginning they were very careful to make sure that I was of the same stylistic bent, and having established that, they never came into town and said, "You have to do this, you have to do that." They wanted absolutely top-quality wines, but they did not ask me to just make an imitation of Taittinger. Imitations are never as good as originals! Where would Picasso be if he had only tried to imitate Renoir?

THAT'S A GREAT APPROACH. BUT HOW DO YOU MAKE THAT HAPPEN OUT IN THE FIELD: PRODUCE TOP-END SPARKLING WINES OF THE HIGHEST QUALITY?

One way is to grow your own grapes. We have evolved into being an organic grower. So our vineyards don't have pesticides or herbicides used in them. Going organic (in 2007) has made a huge difference in the quality of the grapes; little by little, the quality has increased until today it's just off the charts.

WHAT DECISIONS DO YOU MAKE IN THE WEEKS BEFORE YOUR HARVEST? HOW DO YOU DECIDE WHEN TO BRING IN THE GRAPES?

I spend a lot of time walking the vineyards: looking at the grapes, seeing if there are any issues, talking to our vineyard manager, trying to get a sense of what's going on out there. Do things look healthy? Should we be irrigating a little bit or is it time to cut it off?

We harvest sparkling grapes early (around mid-August), so we usually don't see rot or mildew problems, but we might see uneven ripening and decide to do a green harvest.

DO YOU LOOK FOR A CERTAIN pH LEVEL OR TOTAL ACIDITY (TA) OR A CERTAIN BRIX NUMBER BEFORE YOU START HARVESTING?

The truth is, I don't! Of course, we do laboratory analysis, we bring in samples, and do the numbers, but I've been making sparkling wine for thirty-two years now and I always find that my palate tells me to go, or not to go. The numbers give you signals, the lab will tell you whether harvest is on the radar screen or not, but my final picking decisions are based on taste.

IS A SPARKLING WINE HARVEST DIFFERENT FROM A STILL WINE HARVEST?

Yes, it's different because with still wines you have a window of time to harvest. You might say, let's bring in grapes on Tuesday … or … maybe we'll bring them in on Thursday. But with sparkling wines, because they go through a growth spurt just before harvest, you have to be right on top of it. If they are ready on Tuesday, Wednesday's going to be too late or it's not going to be nearly as good.

WHAT HAPPENS IN THAT SHORT PERIOD OF TIME?

If you get a heat spell you can get sugars that are too high; they can move 3° Brix in a week. In sparkling wine, you don't want too much sugar because you also have a secondary fermentation (in the bottle), which adds more alcohol. We are looking for alcohols of 11.2 percent to 11.3 percent in the raw wine, because after the secondary fermentation, they finish around 12.4 percent.

DO YOU HAND PICK OR MACHINE HARVEST YOUR GRAPES?

We are entirely hand picked.

DO YOU USE SMALL BASKETS OR ½-TON BULK BINS?

Most people say that little baskets are much better for the quality of the grapes. But, based on experience at Taittinger in Champagne, we have opted for bins with a large footprint, but are just 18 inches (45.7 cm) tall—something we call "shorties"—so they are ⅓ ton, not ½ ton. We find they're better for the quality of the wine, because you can move them in and out of the vineyards faster—the little baskets take much longer to stack and if the pickers are not careful, if they put one on top of the other, they squish the grapes.

WHAT TIME OF DAY DO YOU PICK?

It depends on the temperature. About 80 to 90 percent of what we pick is harvested at night, because of the cooler temperatures. This gives the grapes a chance to cool off. Our pickers normally start at 2:00 or 3:00 in the morning. They actually prefer this because they don't have to work in the heat of the day. So it's a win/win situation for the grapes and the pickers!

AND THEY'RE BROUGHT IN IMMEDIATELY FOR PROCESSING?

Yes, we have four different vineyard sites within 3½ miles (5.6 km) of the winery. We can load the trucks, and the grapes are ready to be processed within half an hour of being picked.

JUST ONE MORE QUESTION: WHAT DRIVES YOU TO PUT YOURSELF THROUGH THE HARVEST WRINGER EVERY YEAR?

After all this time, I'm still a hands-on winemaker. Sparkling wine is just absolutely what I love to do. I'm still excited to see the first loads that come into the presses. The smell of the grapes and the new fermentations, the blending of the cuvées—it makes my heart beat fast. People ask me if I still have to do it and I tell them I don't have to do it; it's what I want to do.

IS IT CHAMPAGNE OR IS IT SPARKLING WINE?

Sparkling wine is simply wine with bubbles. It can be made anywhere in the world. Champagnes are sparkling wines from the Champagne district of France. Like most French wines, Champagnes are named for the district in which they are grown rather than the grape varieties from which they are made. A wine grown in the Champagne district that wishes to qualify as Champagne is made according to strict local standards. It must be refermented in the bottle (to get those wonderful bubbles), then aged and sold in the same bottle. After years of international suits, France has established that other wine regions can use the same method (Méthode Champenoise or Méthode Traditionelle), but only wines grown in Champagne can be called Champagne. (Note from Eileen Crane: As of 2010, the United States and a few other countries have not signed on to these agreements so there are still some "champagne" designated wines produced in the world.)

There are other ways to add bubbles to a wine:

Charmat process: refermenting a whole cuvée in a pressure tank

Bulk method: injecting CO_2 into a wine as it is being bottled

Typically, only wines made in the traditional Méthode Champenoise are considered "fine" sparkling wines.

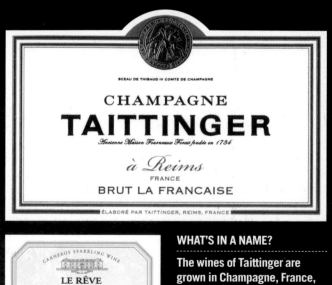

WHAT'S IN A NAME?

The wines of Taittinger are grown in Champagne, France, using the traditional Méthode Champenoise. These sparkling wines are thus qualified to be called Champagne. The American Domaine Carneros wine uses the same grapes and the same production method, but must be called "sparkling wine" because it is not grown in Champagne.

PART II:
MAKING WINE

CHAPTER 6:
ON THE CRUSH PAD

THE THUNDER OF ARRIVING TRUCKS ... THE GNASHING OF STAINLESS STEEL AUGURS ... THE THUMP OF PUMPS MOVING FRESH GRAPE JUICE FROM CRUSHER-STEMMER TO PRESS. FOR A WINEMAKER WHO WAITS ALL YEAR FOR HIS OR HER ONE CHANCE AT FAME AND FORTUNE (OR AT LEAST MAKING *WINE SPECTATOR'S* TOP 100 LIST), THERE IS A VISCERAL THRILL AS FRUIT BEGINS TO ARRIVE ON THE PROCESSING DECK AND THE YEAR'S WINEMAKING BEGINS IN EARNEST.

PROCESSING GRAPES INTO JUICE

Whether you're foot stomping grapes in a garbage can or using the most sophisticated new stainless steel equipment, whether you're making millions of gallons or just a few hundred, the process of turning the just-picked whole grape clusters into fresh grape juice is basically the same. You need to unload and weigh the grapes, evaluate and sort the fruit, remove the stems, delicately crush the berries, and press the juice from the stems, skins, and seeds. The order of the process, and how many steps are taken, depends on whether the wine being made is destined to be red or white, sweet or dry, light and delicate, or rich and robust.

PROCESSING GRAPES FOR WHITE WINES

Grapes headed for dry whites are ideally picked cool or cooled immediately after picking and before processing to minimize availability of harsh phenols when stems are removed during the crushing and pressing process. Because there is no need for color in whites, the process is simple:

1 Grapes are lightly crushed in a stemmer-crusher, which removes the berries from the stems.

2 The resultant thick mixture of flesh, seeds, and skins is then pumped into a press—which typically operates by air pressure—to screen and separate the juice from the seeds and skins.

3 Now is the time for winemakers to analyze the juice for nutrition and health, make corrections (or pray like hell), divide the juice for quality, and bring it to ideal temperature for its next stage: fermentation. Yeast loves temperatures around 85°F (29°C), but to retain best fruit character, 55 to 70°F (13 to 21°C) seems to be the sweet spot.

PROCESSING GRAPES FOR RED WINES

Most red wines are more complex than whites, making for more steps on the crush pad. The biggest difference in processing big dry reds is that the juice has extended contact with the skin and seeds—and in some cases with the stems—before pressing.

1 Red grapes are crushed like whites, but do not go directly to the press. The pulpy part of most red grapes has no color (check this out in the table grapes you buy at the grocery store!) and barely produces a light pink juice if quickly pressed.

2 To obtain deep red/purple hues, the juice sits with the skins and seeds for a period of time to extract color.

3 Unlike whites, which are fermented after pressing, reds are typically inoculated with yeast at this stage to kick-start the initial fermentation (during which the grapes' sugars are converted into alcohol).

4 During this maceration process, the red juice will pick up not only color but also "mouthfeel"—color-stabilizing and mouth-drying tannins—and flavors intense enough to hold up to the most potent, spicy, carnivorous dishes.

5 Some winemakers like to add the stems back into the macerating/fermenting juice for additional textures and flavors, almost replicating the old-fashioned foot-stomping process!

6 When the red wine is deemed to have enough color, flavor, and texture, most of the liquid will be drained off; the remaining seeds and skins are pumped or carried to the press to separate the rest of the raw fermenting wine so it can be moved to a tank or barrel to continue its fermentation.

7 Typically, medium-bodied reds will sit five to ten days between crush and press, but daring winemakers who are looking for gobs of big jammy fruit and mouth-blistering tannins may let the juice, skin, and seeds macerate and ferment for upwards of twenty-five to thirty days.

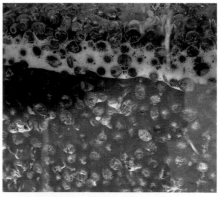

Some winemakers produce light-bodied reds with a delightful candylike nose by employing a technique called carbonic maceration. Here, whole berries undergo fermentation within the closed container of their own skins.

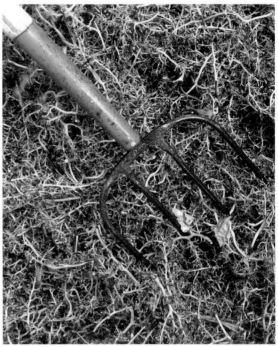

Grapes picked by hand arrive at the crush pad in small picking lugs that must be dumped by hand (above) into larger bins or directly into the stemmer-crusher, while mechanically harvested grapes arrive in large one-ton bulk bins (below) that are then forklifted into the hopper of the destemmer.

The stems that are removed from the grape clusters are sometimes discarded, but more typically are returned to the vineyard, where they are regarded as highly valued organic matter to fertilize the soil and provide nutrition to the vines.

Sorting is the term used for the removal of leaves, twigs, and damaged berries, or what is commonly called MOG (material other than grape), before the grapes are dumped into the destemmer.

When red grapes are finished macerating with their skin and seeds, the partially fermented juice is drained off, while the remaining mixture of seeds and skins—called pomace—is pumped, shoveled, or bucketed out of the tank. More than one hard shoveling soul has succumbed to CO_2 and alcohol fumes at this job.

Processing grapes on the crush pad can be a cold, wet, sticky mess, and the hardest part is cleaning up all the equipment and bins at the end of a long day.

Freshly crushed Cabernet Sauvignon grapes spill from the stemmer-crusher on this production pad.

A typical midsize crush pad showing 1-ton grape bins being dumped into the stemmer-crusher by a forklift.

At this large-scale winery, you may see long processions of trucks lined up each day during harvest, waiting to dump their loads into underground hoppers leading into the stemmer-crusher.

To extract color from the skins, this winery worker is "pumping over," a process that splashes fermenting red grape juice over the "cap" of grape skins that forms at the top of the tank.

THE WINEMAKER'S TOOL BOX

Here is a brief overview of some of the "tricks of the trade" that are used by commercial winemakers to enhance the basic processes that take place on the crush pad.

COLD SOAK

Many Burgundian winemakers, and others using the same Pinot Noir grape, believe greater complexity comes from a prefermentation "cold soak" on the crush pad. This process continues until either natural yeast kicks in and begins the fermentation, or a desirable strain of yeast is added.

WHOLE CLUSTER FERMENTATION

To make lighter reds, winemakers use a technique called "carbonic maceration." Here, whole clusters of unbroken berries are piled into sealed containers to sit, oxygen-free (under CO_2), for five to eight days while natural enzymatic activity magnifies light, candylike smells, contributing to their early "drinkability."

PUNCH DOWN/PUMP OVER

As red wines ferment, CO_2 is trapped inside the skins, causing them to rise and form a "cap." To extract color from the skins and keep the cap from overheating, winemakers remix the skins with the juice by either punching the skins down into the juice or pumping the fermenting juice over the top of the cap.

FREE-RUN JUICE

An extra step between crushing and pressing used to get more acid and higher sugar (and conversely less color and less tannin) in making light, delicate whites and rosés. Once the grapes are crushed and sitting in the press, the first juice is allowed to run off before the press is started; it contains the highest acid and sugar, and the most delicate fruit.

REFRIGERATOR WINES (AND OTHER LUSCIOUS SWEET WINES)

Some sweet wines are made by letting the grapes hang longer (late-harvest dessert wines), drying them indoors (Vin Santo), letting the grapes be attacked by the "noble rot" *Botrytis* (Sauternes), or letting them freeze on the vine (ice wines). But "refrigerator wines" (a term coined by the wine industry's greatest intellectual comedian, Randall Graham of Bonny Doon Vineyards) are made by freezing the water out of fresh grape juice to leave a concentrated, very sweet juice.

Botrytis cinerea, better known as "noble rot," is a fungus that desiccates grapes, causing concentration of sugars and unctuous ripe fruit flavors. The resulting distinctive sweet dessert wines, most notably Sauternes and Trockenbeerenauslese, are often called "the wine of kings."

Although modern winemaking equipment is mostly stainless steel, you may still see old wooden wine presses being used to crush grapes at small wineries, or to decorate the cellars.

Canada's Inniskillin Winery has the ideal conditions needed to produce ice wines, made by allowing the grapes to hang on the vine until they freeze, and then picking them while the water is still frozen and the sugars extremely concentrated.

Sonoma's Ravenswood Winery, which has achieved cult status for its "no wimpy wines" logo and large portfolio of "zin-ful" Zinfandels, makes no bones about its favoritism for big, full-bodied reds.

Although it is now legal in France to blend white and red wines to make rosé, purists use red grapes that are pressed immediately off their skins and seeds, like the most delicate whites, resulting in a light pink color.

The best-known and largest selling light red wines in the world come from Beaujolais, and the youngest and freshest are the Beaujolais Nouveau that are bottled immediately following harvest and rushed to market around November 15th every year to celebrate the end of the harvest season.

Adam and Dianna Lee worked at several small family-owned wineries, learning everything they could about grape growing and winemaking, before starting Siduri Wines in 2004.

INTERVIEW WITH:
ADAM AND DIANNA LEE
SIDURI WINES, SONOMA COUNTY, CALIFORNIA, UNITED STATES

I FIRST MET ADAM LEE ABOUT TWENTY YEARS AGO WHEN I WAS TRYING TO FLOG OFF A FEW BOTTLES OF CHADDSFORD WINE IN SOUTHERN MARKETS AND HE WAS MANAGER OF A FINE WINE STORE IN AUSTIN, TEXAS. WE HAD A GREAT DINNER TOGETHER AT AN EXCITING RESTAURANT OUT IN THE COUNTRYSIDE, DRINKING A MULTITUDE OF WINES, AND SOMEHOW I KNEW WE WOULD CROSS PATHS AGAIN IN OUR WINE CAREERS.

Adam went on to become president of Austin [Texas] Wine & Spirits, did a brief stint in wine wholesale, then became wine buyer for Neiman Marcus in Dallas. There he met his wife, Dianna Novy, and their mutual love of wine eventually led these two self-proclaimed "wine geeks" to California, where they ended up working together at a small winery in the Dry Creek Valley.

Now truly immersed in the wine business, Adam and Dianna decided to invest their meager savings in producing a bit of their own wine—their dream was to make "killer" Pinot Noir—so they started a search for the right grapes. They ended up working a 1-acre (0.4 ha) plot in Anderson Valley, where they dramatically reduced the crop load, made the wine as naturally as possible—using indigenous yeast—purchased French oak barrels, and ultimately produced a grand total of 107 cases of Pinot Noir. The rest is history!

HOW DID YOU GO FROM THAT FIRST SMALL LOT TO OWNING SIDURI WINES AND BEING WIDELY KNOWN TODAY FOR PRODUCING SOME OF THE BEST SINGLE-VINEYARD PINOT NOIRS IN CALIFORNIA?

One evening years ago, Dianna and I heard that the famed wine writer Robert Parker was staying nearby at the Meadowood Resort in Napa Valley. Definitely emboldened by the wine, we pulled a sample of our Pinot Noir, took it to Meadowood, and left it with the concierge for Mr. Parker. The wine ultimately received a 90-point rating in the Wine Advocate, and Siduri just kind of took off from there.

TELL ME ABOUT SIDURI TODAY.

We started Siduri in 1994. Our goal since day one has been to master Pinot Noir by experimenting with a variety of vineyard sources. Each year we purchase fruit from more than twenty top-tier vineyards, stretching from Santa Barbara [California] north to Oregon's Willamette Valley. We turn them into single-vineyard Pinot Noirs to maximize the expression of these very diverse sites. We also have a sister label, Novy Family Winery. Between our two brands we do 15,000 cases, 5,000 under the Novy label.

HOW WOULD YOU DESCRIBE YOUR PHILOSOPHY ABOUT WINEMAKING AND SIDURI IN GENERAL?

Dianna and I make every wine together. We always have. We believe that from each vintage, from each vineyard, there is a Perfect Wine to be made. And when we make a wine, a really outstanding wine, we believe there's a better one out there … somewhere. We continue to strive because the effort is, in and of itself, worthy. Some may argue that this quest sets us up for a winemaking life of dissatisfaction. We acknowledge that and have come to peace with that fact. We are unapologetic roman-

tics both in our personal lives and when it comes to wine and winemaking. It's simply who we are.

HOW DO YOU ACTUALLY GO ABOUT MAKING "THE PERFECT WINE," STARTING WITH THE ARRIVAL OF THE GRAPES ON THE CRUSH PAD?

This is such a special, exciting time. After all your work in the vineyard, after all the anticipation and waiting, things are finally starting. Everything is ahead of us. It's the end of the grapes' life and the beginning of the wines' life. It's also the most critical time, as we are making decisions about the wine that can't be undone later. And

WHAT KINDS OF DECISIONS? WHAT KINDS OF ADJUSTMENTS?

We don't have any of our own vineyards, but we seek out and buy our grapes from exemplary growers such as Clos Pepe Vineyard, Pisoni Vineyard, and Cargasac- chi Vineyard. But even then, things don't always go perfectly. Based on the season, the section of the vineyard, the pecu- liarities of a particular site, we might be considering questions such as, "Will the wine need more concentration, or less? Did we get higher yields than we expected from a particular vineyard, so that we might have to bleed off some of the juice to get more concentration? Or did we get lower yields than expected and have to worry about the wine being over-extracted?" For example, we may have very small berries from a particular vineyard, with a high skin-to- juice ratio, so we might end up with too much alcohol and tannin.

SO WHAT WOULD YOU DO ABOUT THAT?

In part, we just accept it and try to work with it. We change the cold-soak and punch down regimen—doing longer cold soaks and less punch down during fermen- tation so as not to extract too much tannin.

The beginning of the crush is a time of great anticipation and opportunity and excitement.

It's always a give-and-take. You try to work with what the grapes are giving you and make short calls for things that just didn't work out in the vineyard.

In other instances, we might decide to do whole cluster fermentation instead of crushing the berries first. California Pinot Noirs are naturally intensely fruity wines, but they don't always have enough structure. Fermenting whole clusters can add complexity and lift the aromatics so you get sensations such as dried herbs instead of just big fruit; but it's a trade-off because it increases the pH to make the wine softer.

WHAT OTHER KINDS OF DECISIONS ARE YOU MAKING ON THE CRUSH PAD?

We're thinking about tanks and space and where you put the darn grapes. So you need to know how much juice you are going to end up with. Going back to the case of high yields, sometimes we will bleed off (in the classic Saignée method), about 20 percent of the free-run juice to increase the concentration of the remaining 80 percent. We're always thinking about where things fit and what type of fermentation vessel is best.

WHAT OTHER CRITICAL POINTS ARE YOU CONSIDERING?

We're also concerned about peak temperatures, with temps getting too warm and out of whack in the fermentations. And we almost always do a cold soak, for up to five days, and during this time we keep things under dry ice so they stay cold and don't start fermenting. Then we make a decision about whether we ferment by using indigenous yeast or by adding a commercial strain.

WITH ALL THESE CRUCIAL DECISIONS TAKING PLACE ON THE CRUSH PAD, ARE YOU ALWAYS THERE?

Either Dianna or I will be there. We're a teamed pair of winemakers. Given how spread out our vineyards are, if I'm out observing grapes elsewhere, then Dianna will be on the crush pad. We're always calling each other with information, such as "Wow, we only got three tons instead of five …"

DO YOU FIND IT'S THE SAME EVERY YEAR? HOW DOES THE PROCESS VARY YEAR TO YEAR?

Like every winery, there are certain things we always do. For instance, we sort every bin of grapes that comes in from the vineyard. But some years we don't have much to sort out, so it goes very quickly.

Other years it's very slow because you have to sort every berry. And some years there are things that are just totally out of your control, things you couldn't possibly anticipate. For example, in 2008 there were fires on the Sonoma coast and we were worried that the grapes had picked up smoke characteristics. We called everyone we knew in Australia, where they had just had a similar problem, and ended up using a proprietary filtration procedure developed over there. That's not something you deal with every year!

ANY OTHER WORRIES YOU HAVE WHILE OUT THERE ON THE CRUSH PAD?

We worry about visitors who come to the winery. They always want to see the crush. But in reality, the crush pad is cold and wet and messy and slippery (not to mention full of bees), so you're always worried about their safety. You want them to see all the excitement of a new crush, but you don't want anybody to get hurt.

YOU MENTIONED THE MESSY PHYSICAL SIDE OF THE CRUSH. HOW ABOUT THE EMOTIONAL SIDE OF THE CRUSH?

At the beginning of the crush you are full of exhilaration. You have the mind-set of an artist who is getting ready to create something that will go on long after the harvest is over. It is a time of great anticipation and opportunity and excitement.

Then, when the crush begins, you live off adrenaline. Our harvest hours are often from 4 a.m. to 7 p.m., and you do that seven days a week for about six weeks. And during that whole time, you are cranked up, adrenaline pumping, full of confidence that you are going to get it right and anxiety that you might have missed a trick.

Then, at the end of the crush, when you're cleaning up and putting things away, you are simply exhausted. And you have a great sense of relief that it's over, you did it again, you have a cellar full of new wine. It doesn't get much better than that!

Siduri was named for the Babylonian goddess of wine, who in Babylonian mythology held the wine of eternal life. You will find her on all the Siduri labels. Siduri produces more than twenty-five different Pinot Noirs, most from single vineyards, representing the largest Pinot Noir focus of any winery in California.

SIDURI™

PISONI VINEYARD
SANTA LUCIA HIGHLANDS PINOT NOIR

2008

ALC. 14.7% BY VOL.

THE VINTNER'S MARKETPLACE

There are several good resources available to home winemakers who want to purchase fruit for winemaking:

LOCAL WINERIES AND VINEYARDS: Grapes are being grown in just about every region in the world today with a moderate climate. Seek out wineries and vineyards in your area and find out if they are willing to sell small quantities and what grapes are available. Contact them well before harvest time and be prepared to pay the going price! (*Hint:* If you volunteer to be a harvest helper, you can learn the process at the same time.)

FRESH MARKETS: Every good-size city has an Italian market or other fresh market where some vendor specializes in wine grapes. Fresh grapes are available from various sources two times a year. In March the Southern Hemisphere harvest is in full swing and in October grapes are plentiful in the Northern Hemisphere.

HOME WINEMAKING SHOPS: If you're not successful in finding fresh grapes, look for a small business in your area that sells home winemaking (and probably brewing) supplies. In addition to bottles, corks, and capsules, they may have alternatives such as crushed grapes, grape juice, frozen juice, and/or juice concentrate.

WINE GROUPS: If all else fails, join a local wine group or a local chapter of a wine society; you'll find other wine aficionados and home winemakers, along with plenty of advice about where to find grapes and winemaking supplies in your area.

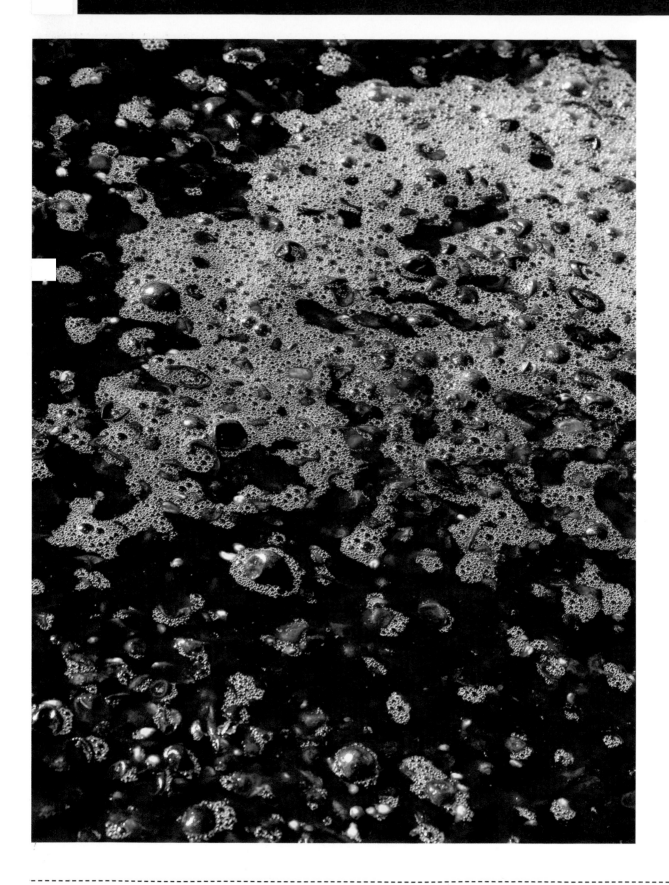

IT WAS THE FALL OF 1982. IT WAS WELL PAST LATE. I WAS SITTING CROSS-LEGGED ATOP A STAINLESS STEEL TANK ABOUT 20 FEET (6.1 M) OFF THE GROUND, SPRAYING COLD WATER DOWN THE SIDES ONTO A FLOWERED BLANKET THAT WRAPPED THE TANK. A BIG WINDOW FAN WAS BLOWING ACROSS THE BLANKET, EVAPORATING THE WATER AND (HOPEFULLY) PULLING HEAT OUT OF THE METAL TANK WALLS.

CHAPTER 7:
FERMENTATION: GRAPES INTO WINE

As the sun began to peek in through the cellar door, I painfully straightened my legs and climbed down the ladder to pull a sample and check the temperature of the wine in the tank. It was my first Chardonnay vintage in this region and I had no jacketed tanks to control temperatures. Fermentation had taken off like a rocket the evening before, and I feared that overheating would kill the yeast and I would lose all the fruit characteristics of those beautiful grapes. This was simply not an option.

My decision to wrap the tank and sit there all night dripping cold water saved the day—and the Chardonnay. After I got some sleep, I tied blankets around the rest of the tanks, made drip lines around the top of each one, and set up an array of fans.

And then the moment I could afford it, I bought jacketed polypropylene-cooled tanks so I never again had to think about ruining another batch of wine because of overheating during fermentation.

This new red wine from Burgundy has just begun its fermentation. Over the next few weeks the "must" will absorb flavor and color and a great deal more from the skins and seeds as it macerates and ferments.

FACTORS IN FERMENTATION

Fermentation is the process that converts grape juice into wine. On one hand, it is a simple process whereby yeast consumes the sugar in the fresh juice and converts it into alcohol. On the other hand, there are details that make it one of the most critical times in a wine's life. Although fermentation will occur on its own with wild yeast, most winemakers want to control it to achieve the character and style of the wine they wish to make. The critical factors in fermentation are yeast, temperature, nutrition, and bacteria.

YEAST

Both white and red wines go through a "primary" fermentation when yeast converts sugar into alcohol and CO_2. White wines are typically fermented in a neutral container such as a used wooden barrel or stainless steel tank, after the juice has been pressed off the skins.

Red wines are initially fermented on the grape skins, seeds, and occasionally stems. This is done to extract textural qualities and color from the skins, and because tannins extracted from skins, seeds, and stems help stabilize color and contribute to the wine's aging potential. (For more on tannins, see "Tech Talk on Tannins" later in this chapter.)

Commercial Yeasts

There is a big selection of commercial yeasts available that give winemakers a degree of control during fermentations. Particular strains are selected because they bring out more or less fruit character, leave a residual sugar (or not), efficiently produce higher alcohol (or not), and other desirable (or not) characteristics.

Native Yeasts

Not surprisingly, there is a great philosophical debate between winemakers who add such selected yeast strains versus those who rely on the serendipity of Mother Nature. Such native yeast strains can be found just about anywhere in a winery—in the air, on wall surfaces, on the processing equipment, in new barrels, in floor drains, on the waxy skins of the grapes. The dominant issue with these wild strains is that they are often unpredictable.

One of the most controversial native yeasts is call "Brett" (*Brettanomyces*), known, loved and hated—depending on one's point of view—either for adding brilliant complexity or for contributing "barnyard" and occasional iodine-like smells and flavors. But even the nicest, most popular cultured yeast will produce off-characteristics (like rotten eggs) if stressed during fermentation.

TEMPERATURE

Temperature is a very important factor during fermentation, and in determining what the wine will be like after the fermentation is finished. Low-temperature fermentations tend to preserve fresh, fruity smells, but when temps drop below 45°F (7.2°C), yeast become very sluggish, might arrest, and leave the partially fermented juice (called "must") open to bacterial infection.

Higher temperature fermentations tend to bring out riper fruit characteristics, until they approach a critical point around 120°F (48.9°C) and yeast begin to die off, blow off most of the pretty fruit, and, again, leave the wine open to infections.

Wineries that ferment large lots, especially in warm climates, control must temperature by circulating a coolant through jacketed tanks. One of the challenges for wineries in cool climates is that small vessels might be too cold for yeast to become active. Of course, the benefit is that once started, the must might not generate enough heat to need temperature control. In most wineries, temperatures are monitored at least once daily during the active fermentations.

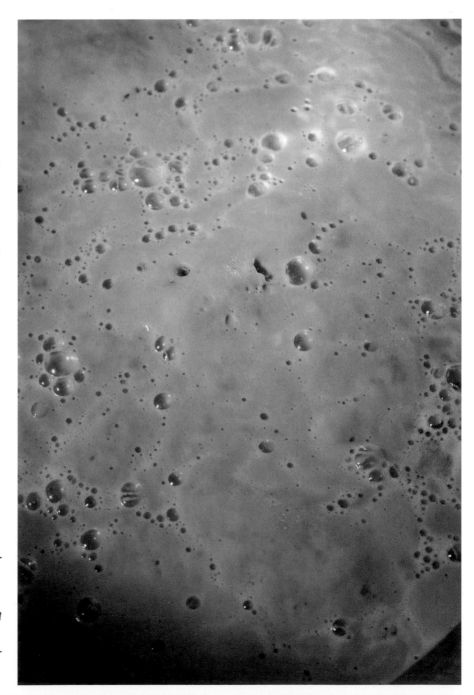

This "starter" culture of yeast is rehydrated, activated, and about to be added to a tank of fresh juice to begin fermentation.

Red wine fermenters have dimple jackets through which a coolant flows; multiple valves for sampling, mixing, and draining; and access doors for removal of skins and seeds.

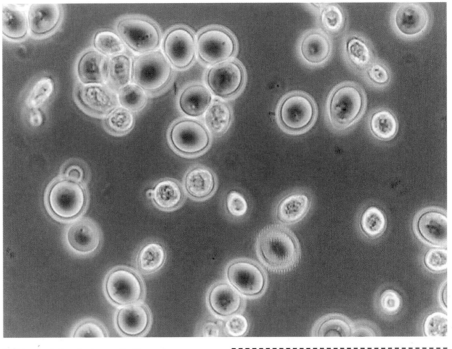

Microscopic picture of budding, reproducing yeast, photographed through a microscope by Vinquiry, an independent wine-testing laboratory in Sonoma County, California.

NUTRITION

Yeast needs appropriate nutrition to function in a sweet acidic juice and produce the desired smells, flavors, and level of alcohol. Although we think of sugar as being the main food for yeast, there is a mix of nutrients such as oxygen and nitrogen that keeps yeast reproducing, making desirable smells, flavors, and alcohol. Conversely, undernourished "stressed" yeast might produce off-characteristics or die off and let an undesirable strain take over.

BACTERIA

Wines that are too high in acid and lack complexity (primarily reds, but also some over-acidic whites) are often encouraged to go through a "secondary" malolactic fermentation. In this process, the malolactic bacteria (ML) convert malic acid (think apple) to CO_2 and lactic acid (think milk). Thus, the wine becomes softer in the mouth with the added flavor effects of this fermentation.

There are various commercial ML cultures available, but again, there is the perpetual debate between "au natural" and controlled fermentation. Many winemakers are wary of wild ML bacteria (which can come in with the grapes or just linger around the winery) because some produce amines as a by-product and cause the classic red wine headache. Also, the circumstances that are ideal for ML are just as suitable for creating vinegar and accommodating other "bad" bacteria!

Wild yeast, bacteria, and other microorganisms are among the scary variables winemakers learn to live with. They are typically kept in control by some combination of keeping a clean shop, reducing oxygen exposure, maintaining high acids (especially in white wines), keeping the cellar cool, and assiduous use of sulphur dioxide (better known as SO_2, sulfite, or *meta*).

WINEMAKER'S FAQ'S ABOUT FERMENTATION

Fermentation is an area that confounds new winemakers because there are so many variables. Some of the answers come from studying the science of the fermentation process, but most will come from experience (and trial and error). Here are a few standard questions that may be asked by new winemakers going through the process for the first time.

At Chaddsford Winery in southeastern, Pennsylvania, fermentation temperatures are closely monitored in jacketed stainless steel tanks with precision gauges.

HOW DO YOU MAKE A HIGH ALCOHOL WINE VERSUS A LOW ALCOHOL WINE?

It's all about the sugar content in the must. Regions with a long, warm growing season tend to produce grapes with higher sugars and, therefore, have greater alcohol potential. Cooler regions tend to produce grapes with lower sugars and, consequently, have lower alcohol potential. Cool regions that strive for higher alcohols need to crop lightly and let early ripening varieties hang on the vine longer to increase sugar content in the grapes.

IF THERE'S NOT ENOUGH SUGAR, CAN YOU ADD SUGAR?

It depends on where you live. Adding sugar is called chaptalization. It is typically illegal to add sugar during the winemaking process in a warm winegrowing area that produces high sugars, although adding a sweet concentrate (made by removing water from the must to concentrate the sugars) or reserve (unfermented grape juice added after the original fermentation) is not uncommon. Currently, chaptalization is prohibited in Australia, Austria, California, Italy, and South Africa. It is permitted in some regions of France and the United States and in Germany (except for certain wine types).

When fermentation is complete, the finished wine is racked off the yeast sediments. This jug shows sediments that have settled out, with a bit of clear wine at the top.

IF YOU FERMENT ALL THE SUGAR OUT (TO GET ALCOHOL), HOW DO YOU MAKE SWEET WINES?

Winemakers with good equipment are able to stop yeast activity while the wine is still sweet by chilling the must in a jacketed tank. Those who rely on luck pray for a sudden change in the weather so they can let the cold outside air into the cellar to do the chilling. Other tools available are racking (or transferring) the unfinished wine off as much of the yeast as possible before chilling and shocking the yeast into inactivity with a modest sulfite addition. Another solution is to add sugar (where legal; see previous question) or a sweet reserve or concentrate just before bottling.

A cellar worker at Château Ausone in Bordeaux, France, racks free-run raw wine that has finished its fermentation and is en route to its next step, barrel aging.

TECH TALK ON TANNINS

"Tannin" is one of those wine-speak words everybody knows but few people understand. You will hear "tannins" mentioned in discussions about wine processing, fermentation, and aging—or maybe even tea!

Tannins are by definition astringent, bitter plant polyphenols that bind and precipitate or shrink proteins and other organic compounds. In winemaking, they stabilize red color, combat browning, contribute astringency and bitterness, and act as antioxidants. The astringency from tannins is what causes the dry and puckery feeling in the mouth when drinking certain wines.

Tannins are picked up when grape juice is in contact with the skins, seeds, and stems, before and during fermentation. They are also picked up from new barrels during barrel aging. The destruction or modification of tannins over time plays an important role in the (bottle) aging of wines.

For the winemaker, tannin management is a constant juggling act. The type and quantity of available tannins are determined by grape variety, vintage conditions, production techniques (such as cold soak or extended maceration on skins, seeds, and stems), fermentation style, and barrel aging. Desirable fine, grainy tannins are softened by exposure to oxygen (via racking/splashing the wine) and by micro-oxidation through the staves of a barrel. Harsh "green" tannins, often acquired from underripe grapes, are addressed by adding fining agents such as egg white and gelatin, which attach to and remove the offending element or material.

TANNIN IN THE TANKS
The author's son, Tannin Miller, at 1½ years old, passing time while dad makes his first vintage at Chaddsford Winery in 1982. This image was used on a cover of *Wines & Vines* the following year.

INTERVIEW WITH:
MARC KENT
BOEKENHOUTSKLOOF, FRANSCHHOEK, SOUTH AFRICA

THE ONLY CHALLENGING PART ABOUT TALKING TO MARC KENT WAS LEARNING TO SAY THE NAME "BOEKENHOUTSKLOOF"! ANOTHER INTERESTING, NEW TOPIC TO EXPLORE WAS HIS FASCINATION WITH AND USE OF SYRAH, WHICH HAS ALWAYS BEEN TRADITIONALLY A RHÔNE VARIETAL TO ME. BUT MARC IS PART OF A RISING TIDE OF YOUNG, ENERGETIC WINEMAKERS IN SOUTH AFRICA WHO ARE FOCUSING ON PRODUCING SMALL LOTS OF HIGH-QUALITY SYRAH AND OTHER RHÔNE VARIETALS—WINES THAT ARE GETTING HIGH MARKS FROM CRITICS AND GROWING MEDIA ATTENTION.

Marc Kent—who once was on track to become a pilot with the South African Air Force until the changing political landscape derailed that option—is both winemaker for and a partner in Boekenhoutskloof, a South African Cape winery founded in 1996 in the Franschhoek Valley. Besides the main label, this 125,000-case winery makes wines under the Chocolate Block, Wolftrap, and Porcupine Ridge brands. In addition to Syrah, Marc also grows and makes wine from Cabernet Sauvignon, Cabernet Franc, Grenache, Sémillon, and Viognier.

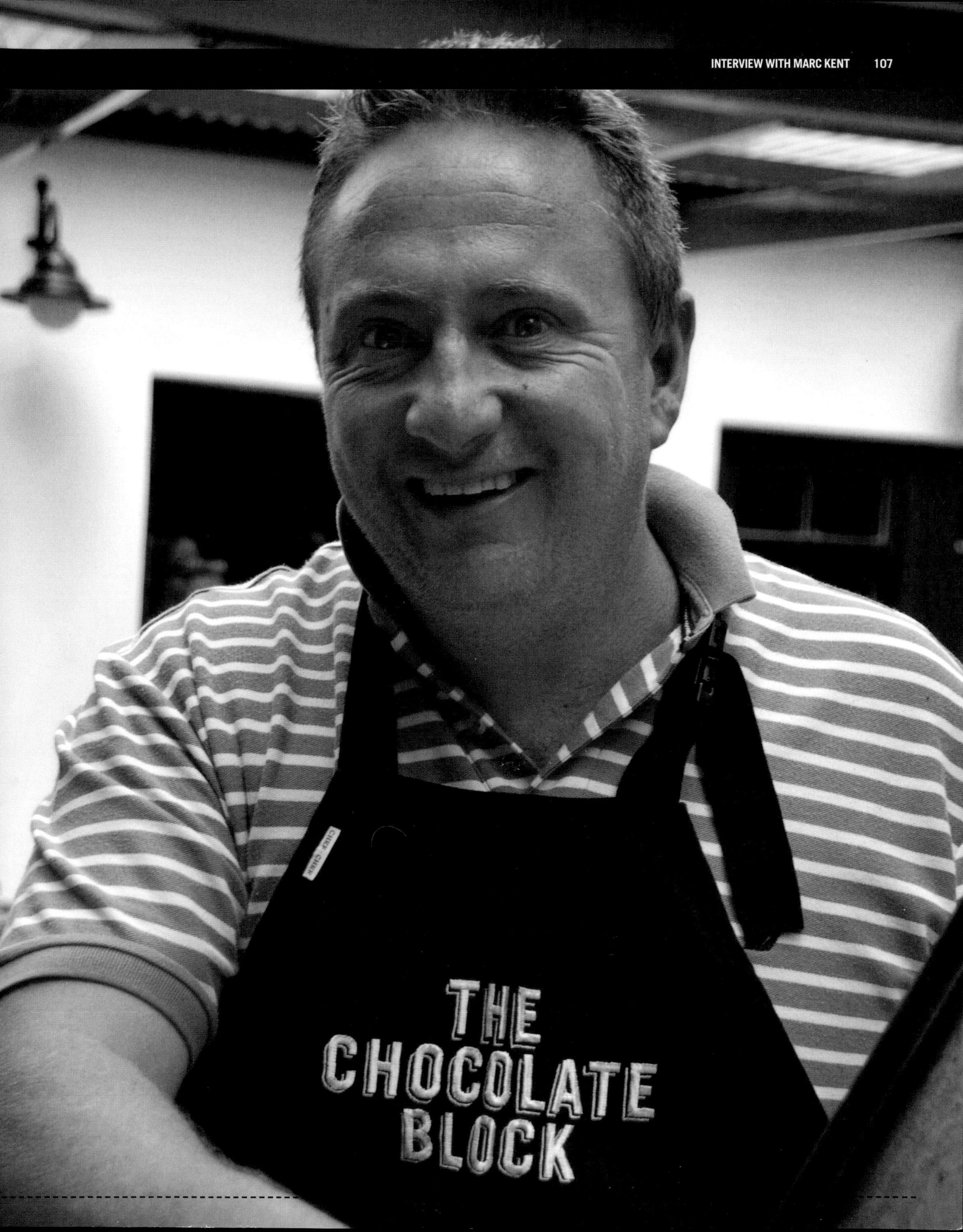
THE
CHOCOLATE
BLOCK

MARC, IN MY OPINION YOU CARRY THE FLAG FOR SOUTH AFRICAN WINES. WHAT'S YOUR BACKGROUND THAT LED TO THIS POSITION?

I landed in the wine business completely by accident. In the late 1980s, I had a stint with the South African Air Force, but the government suspended operations at the flight school before I ever got a chance to fly. So I started working in restaurants, trying to make money to get over to Europe. And while I was waiting tables at one place, I got hooked on wine by the owner, who had an amazing cellar that he was incredibly generous with. After growing up in a home where no wine was consumed, suddenly here I was drinking many of the great wines of the world.

THAT'S QUITE AN INTRODUCTION!

Yes, and then one day he just said to me, "Why don't you go to wine school?" And I thought, wow, that sounds like a cool idea. So I applied and ended up going to Eisenberg Agricultural College in Stellenbosch, where I got a three-year undergraduate diploma in cellar technology. Next thing I knew, I was given an opportunity to join up with a partnership of wine enthusiasts who were committed to the future of South Africa.

AND THEY HAD A WINERY?

They had bought a small farm and homestead known as Boekenhoutskloof, which dates back to 1776, situated about forty minutes northeast of Cape Town. And they wanted to restore it and establish a new vineyard-planting program. They had a history of making wine; in fact, they'd made wine since the 1940s and 1950s, but never producing under their own label. So I joined them and started the planting program. In 1996 we produced our first wine, about 6,000 bottles. Today we produce about 3,000,000.

HOW DOES THAT FIT INTO THE WORLD OF SOUTH AFRICAN WINES? AND HOW DO SOUTH AFRICAN WINES FIT INTO TODAY'S GLOBAL WORLD OF WINES?

You could say that South Africa is the oldest of the "New World" countries, because we have a history of winemaking that dates back to the late seventeenth century. But the world market really only opened up to us after the 1994 election, in the years of Nelson Mandela and the Rainbow Nation.

Boekenhoutskloof winemaker Marc Kent is among the winemakers in California, Italy, and other countries who have reverted to the use of concrete tanks—once considered outdated—because he feels they provide more consistent temperatures to his fermenting wines.

Did you know that globally, South Africa is the world's ninth largest producer? We have about a quarter million acres (101,171 ha) under vine. Stylistically, I think we fall somewhere between the elegance of the Old World and the power of the New World.

Our climate is very Mediterranean. In the Western Cape, where the wine production is concentrated—90 percent of the country's vineyards are within a three-hour radius—we have warm dry summers and cold wet winters. In Franschhoek, where Boekenhoutskloof is, we are particularly wet, with more than eight feet (2.4 m), of rain a year, concentrated in the wet months from June to August.

HOW WOULD YOU DESCRIBE SOUTH AFRICAN WINES?

Anyone who comes to South Africa can see that as a nation there is an incredible sort of warmth and generosity of spirit. And I think you'll see that in the wines as well. They are very much warm-climate wines, rich and full textured. And I think our strength is Syrah, and Syrah blends, with a spicy aromatic profile. But we are different from the New World model, which has the sort of power that jumps out of the glass and punches you in the nose.

HOW ABOUT YOUR OWN WINES? WHAT IS THE PROFILE YOU ARE LOOKING FOR?

Big, up-front fruit. Black currant, or berry flavors, cloves, pepper. Besides the fruit, we emphasize texture. A lot of nuance, a nice richness. Supple and soft, but not overly acidic or tannic.

LET'S TALK ABOUT FERMENTATIONS AND HOW YOU FERMENT TO GET SOME OF THESE CHARACTERISTICS.

Our approach is very hands-on. We work a lot with wild yeast and natural fermentations, especially with the reds. We don't have any mechanical [splashing] systems, so we pump-over everything in the cellar. Everything is done manually with a team of workers sitting on the top of tanks doing the pump-overs, doing the rack and returns.

We do not acidify [add acid], so we rely on natural acidity, often at higher pH ranges. We rely on tannins to help fill in, to give us more "mouthfeel."

The beautiful Boekenhoutskloof winery entices visitors to enjoy the view from an outdoor patio overlooking the Franschhoek Valley.

PLEASE BE MORE SPECIFIC: HOW DO YOU HANDLE WHITE AND RED FERMENTATIONS?

With whites we want the fermentation to be prolonged without stressing the yeast. So we use cooler fermentations—in tanks—to preserve more primary fruit flavors, about 12 to 13°C (53.6 to 55.4°F). In barrels, sometimes a little bit warmer, maybe 14°C (57.2°F). Below that range, the yeast tends to stress.

To be even more specific, there are actually two different ways we can go, depending on the grape and style of the wine. In a light wine such as Sauvignon Blanc, we work at cool temperatures. Our goal is to preserve the fruit and get its beautiful aromatic profile into the bottle, so we really try to limit the exposure to oxygen. This is a style of wine that is made for early consumption.

But with Sémillon, one of the whites in our premium range, we work in the opposite direction: We start by fermenting on the skins for three to four days, like a red, to extract a lot of tannin and give the wine more texture. We do three pump-overs a day. Then, halfway through the fermentation, when we have the potential alcohol, we press it off and finish the fermentation in new barrels, at warmer temperatures. That's how we get these amazingly structured white wines with developed character—wines that age much longer, which are just starting to look interesting after five or six years in the bottle.

SO YOU ARE, IN EFFECT, TREATING THE SÉMILLON LIKE A RED?

Yes, except we don't want it to go through a malolactic fermentation. Sémillon is inherently low in acidity and we don't want to lose any acidity during ML fermentation. As soon as the primary fermentation is done, we turn the temperature down to 5°C (41°F)—it's all fermented in a cold facility so we can cool the whole building—which inhibits any malolactic activity.

THAT'S FASCINATING—NOW I WANT TO GO OUT AND TRY YOUR WHITES. BUT YOU DIDN'T MENTION WHICH TYPE OF YEAST YOU USE ON THE WHITES.

With almost all of our whites, we use cultured yeast.

BUT NOT THE REDS?

No, stylistically, we are a lot more experimental with the reds and open to natural or wild yeast fermentation. All of the premium Syrah is done with wild yeast.

AT WHAT TEMPERATURES DO YOU FERMENT THE REDS?

We tend to ferment at slightly warmer temperatures to get those richer, fuller profiles. We usually get them up to around 28 to 30°C (82.4 to 86°F). I've had some running to 32° or 33°C (89.6° or 91.4°F). For our premium reds we do all the work in concrete open-top vessels.

I'VE NEVER WORKED WITH CONCRETE VESSELS. TELL ME ABOUT THEM.

If I could redesign the whole fermentation shed over again, I would do everything in concrete. It is an amazing material. We get a far more even temperature distribution and far cleaner fermentation curves than with stainless steel tanks.

HOW ABOUT YOUR MACERATION PERIOD? HOW LONG ARE YOUR WINES SITTING ON THE SKINS AND SEEDS?

And stems! Sometimes, to increase tannins, we might throw 20 to 30 percent of the stems into the fermentation vessel. As for the period, we let them sit for about two weeks. On the real premium level we do some barrel fermentations where we ferment the reds inside the barrel, on the skins, and those we can leave for well over a month.

HOW DO YOU "MIX" THEM IN THE BARREL SINCE YOU CAN'T PUMP OVER OR PUNCH DOWN?

We have a rolling mechanism, so you roll the barrels instead of giving them a pumpover. We actually crush right into the bungholes in the barrels and then when the wine is fermenting, we rotate the barrels. And this keeps the skins wet. After the fermentation period, we drain the free-run juice and then the cooper removes the head of the barrel. We take out the skins and press them. It's very labor-intensive, but we make awesome wines in that style.

The Boekenhoutskloof farm, founded in 1776, is one of the oldest in the Franschhoek Valley of South Africa.

THAT'S QUITE AN OPERATION. HOW ABOUT YOUR BIGGER LOTS, THE ONES IN TANKS? DO YOU PUMP THOSE OVER, PUNCH DOWN, OR USE ROTATING TANKS?

No, no, never. Not rotating tanks! I like winemakers to be physically in contact with the tanks. Yes, it's a novelty at first, but when you're sitting on a tank, in the middle of the night, spraying the cap, with the fermenting must running over your hands you can understand more about it than you can from a scent. You can feel the temperature, you can see the color, you can smell the flavors. It is all right there. It's amazing.

A worker punches down the cap of skins and seeds covering a lot of fermenting wine at Boekenhoutskloof winery near Cape Town, South Africa.

to get ML over as quickly as possible—and that's safe winemaking—but I don't mind the wines being idle in the cellar. If it's too cool for the ML to start naturally, if the ML is inhibited, then in the spring it will just start up again. And I'm not worried about that.

WHAT DOES WORRY YOU? ARE YOU WORRIED ABOUT YEAST OR BACTERIAL INFECTIONS DURING FERMENTATION? ABOUT BRETT (*BRETTANOMYCES*)?

No, not too much. We've got quite the advanced selection processes. We monitor, we watch what's going on. I can't say we've never had a tank with VA (vinegar) or some bacteria, but that's all a part of the winemaking game.

As for Brett, well, that was sort of the buzzword a few years ago. And I think we've become too sensitive to it. Once I did an experiment with about three hundred people filing through the winery, and I asked them to taste a wine with Brett and fill out a form. It was split right down the middle—50 percent of them couldn't identify it. They weren't bothered by it at all. I thought that was very interesting.

ANY FINAL WORDS ON FERMENTATION?

I'm happy when it is all over!
We use a lot of unconventional practices here, and occasionally we lose a barrel or two. We probably have two and a half thousand barrels in our program, so losing one here or there is not really a major deal. I operate under the old adage, where there's no risk, there's no reward.

In winemaking one needs to be prudent and sensible, but for me, using techniques that are not conventional makes it a more interesting process, and the resulting products more interesting.

MARC, I THINK YOU'VE GIVEN A NEW DEFINITION TO "HANDS-ON" WINEMAKING! NOW, ONE LAST SUBJECT, HOW ABOUT MALOLACTIC FERMENTATIONS? DO YOU USE CULTURED ML?

I've experimented with it in the past, but we tend to veer away from inoculating the wines with ML because I think there's enough ambient culture in the cellar. I know that a lot of winemakers are in a hurry

PART OF A VINTNER'S JOB IS TO SHOW GUESTS THROUGH THE SCRUBBED CLEAN CELLARS, IMPRESSING THEM WITH ROWS OF BLOND BARRELS, RANKS OF SPARKLING TANKS, PUMPS LINED UP IN PERFECT ORDER. WE MAKE SURE THEY KNOW HOW EXACTING AND DIFFICULT THE WORK IS. WE STOP TO EXAMINE THE SOPHISTICATED ARRAY OF DIGITAL SCREENS, SANITARY CLAMPS, GAUGES, AND FILTERS.

Back in the day when cellars were dark and only lit by candle or lantern, the facets on a silver "taste vin" (as pictured) reflected the light and gave the winemaker insights into the color and clarity of the wine.

CHAPTER 8:
CELLAR WORK

Many times a guest will offer compliments on a particular wine. When this happens to me, I usually stop to gather my thoughts so I can explain how the wine in question was made. Inevitably, my cellarmaster, Jim Osborn, strolls by at that moment, smiles, says "hello," and unknowingly deflates my ego. Then I am compelled to introduce my right- (and occasionally left-) hand man. "This is my cellarmaster," I say. "He does what I get all the credit for doing."

After the excitement and energizing rush of picking and pressing are over … after the fermentations have magically transformed grape juice into wine … before the romance of barrel aging takes place, there is an in-between time in the cellar when the wines begin the "cleaning up" process. This is when their personalities are developing and their foibles are resolving, when they are studied, moved, poked, prodded, tasted, analyzed, and blended into a final version of the winemaker's vision (which likely began many long months ago). This is an unglamorous time of routine tasks and methodical procedures, and the front line of defense for the winemaker is a hardworking cellarmaster and cellar crew.

Wineries use various types of filters to remove unwanted solid material from wines. This one is a "plate and frame filter," or a "pad filter," that removes various size particles by passing wine through cellulose pads.

Although some wineries are set up to move wine by gravity or through overhead pipelines, most transfer wines by using a series of pumps and hoses.

Cellarmasters, cellar dwellers, cellar rats, hose pullers, hose jockeys—whatever these hardworking members of the winemaking team are called—they have a big job to do. Over the course of days, weeks, and months, the wines slowly evolve and become better defined before they are blended and bottled months or years later. This is what we call cellar work. It's about understanding the wine, its history, and why it tastes and looks like it does. But it's also about machines and equipment and many routine, often tedious cellar processes and procedures.

Winemaker's Disclaimer: Not all winemakers "interfere" with the wines in their cellar, and not all wines are subjected to the techniques described.

MOVING THE WINE ALONG

In our winemaking journey we have gone from grapes to raw wine, but there is still a lot to be done before the wines are "finished." In comparison to the short crush and fermentation periods, ongoing cellar work accounts for a long period in the wine's life, from several months to years.

TOPPING UP

Topping up means keeping all containers full. When fermentation ends, wine volume decreases as CO_2 begins to escape and liquid evaporates. Keeping tanks and barrels topped up is critical to minimize oxidation because oxygen and certain oxygen-loving microbes can cause browning of the wine, sherrylike flavors, and vinegar. It is important to top each container with the same wine (so as not to change its character), so a small container of each wine must be kept in the cellar for this purpose, and that container must be topped up, too!

RACKING

Racking involves transferring wines from one container to another via gravity or the use of pumps and hoses. It is done to separate raw wine from sediments after settling or cold stabilizing, to increase oxygen contact or aerate for off-smells (called a "splash rack"), to fit the wine into a barrel or tank that can be topped up, or to move it into a particular container or room with appropriate storage conditions.

COLD STABILIZING

Cold stabilization is done to encourage precipitation of tartrates (natural crystals of tartaric salts, potassium and calcium bitartrate) before bottling. These sediments, which look like tiny shards of glass, appear only after a period of time or low temperature. Cold stabilization is done by either chilling the wines in winter by opening the cellar windows or by using mechanical refrigeration and seeding with cream of tartar (potassium bitartrate) if necessary. The winemaker's goal is for tartrates to drop out in the barrel or tank rather than in the bottle after it is purchased.

FINING

Fining is a process used to remove undesirable characteristics (such as browning, bitterness, or haziness) by adding appropriate materials to the wine. These materials then attach to and remove the offending element. Because there is no such thing as a perfect solution for making this type of amendment, every winemaker has preferences (or abhorrences) for various fining agents because each is notorious for affecting aspects of the wine other than the one being targeted. Egg white fining, for instance, is a gentle way to reduce bitterness and browning; bentonite, a clay material, is commonly used to remove excess protein.

FILTERING

Filtering is the removal of solid particles or microorganisms from wine through the use of various methods and types of equipment. Filters commonly used in winemaking range from large diatomaceous earth filters used for rough filtration, to workhorse plate and frame filters where wine is passed through cellulose pads, to centrifuges that spin the wine until heavy sediments are thrown out, to membrane cartridges with absolute pore size capable of retaining the tiniest bacteria. Some (dry wine) winemakers prefer minimal or no filtration at all because they fear the process will also remove colors, flavors, and other "good" stuff.

EXTREME/UBER-WINEMAKING

Every day, science provides new and wonderful potential winemaking aids. There is even a style of filter that has been used to remove the smoke character that appeared in wines made from grapes that were grown near a wildfire. There is an experimental process that uses CO_2 for extracting color and removing harsh and grassy characteristics from fresh grapes. In time, some of these new processes will become commonplace in the cellar.

OTHER ADDITIONS AND AMENDMENTS

From the moment fresh grapes hit the processing deck to immediately before a wine is bottled, winemakers make constant decisions about whether, how much, and when to add various materials. For example, sulfites are commonly added to preserve color and discourage unwanted microorganisms. Deficiencies in acidity, sugar, and/or tannin can also be addressed through appropriate additions. There are a number of options available to winemakers, and every winemaker has opinions on such matters.

Over and above the winemaker, every wine-producing region has established a set of regulations regarding how, how much, and what materials may be used. Some examples:

■ It is illegal to add sugar in some areas.
■ There are legal limits for sulfite additions (measured in parts per million, PPM) in all areas.
■ Color deficiency may be corrected by adding a super-concentrate grape extract in some areas, but not in others.
■ Copper sulfate, a heavy metal used to remove off-odors in wine, is considered a health hazard when it exceeds set limits.

TRACKING THE WINE

The mechanical jobs of the cellar move the wine from point "A" to point "B," but at the same time these operations are being done, the wines must also be followed, analyzed, and recorded so that good decisions can be made, now and in the future.

OBSERVING

The most readily available tools (and many would say the most important) in any winery are the winemaker's eyes, nose, and mouth. Although the cellar is full of equipment, and the laboratory can measure hundreds of quantifiable characteristics, there is simply no substitute for experience and sensory evaluation. Every wine in the cellar must be looked at, smelled, tasted, and evaluated to see whether it is at the right point in its development at any particular time. For the winemaker, this is an ongoing and time-consuming job, but also an exhilarating one. It's a time to close one's eyes, think about the original vision for the wine, and "use the force, Luke" before taking the next appropriate action.

Jim Osborn, cellarmaster at Chaddsford Winery, uses a "thief" to pull a barrel sample for the lab. Such glass pipettes are also commonly used for barrel tasting with consumers.

SAMPLING

Although most important decisions about a wine's development are made by tasting, they must be backed up by good information. For standard evaluation, lab tests, and occasional trials to be done, accurate representations of the wine in question must be carefully pulled. This can be very challenging if a cuvée has not yet been assembled (through blending of various lots) or is in multiple containers, where each separate barrel or tank has its own unique characteristics.

RECORD KEEPING

Every wine region has its own legal requirements for keeping track of what has been done with each wine in the cellar. And the winery itself needs good records to follow a wine's history and create future procedures and protocols. Whether the facility is completely computerized or the winemaking team relies on handwritten journals, it is a task that must be done on a daily basis.

MAINTAINING THE CELLAR

Many people begin working in a cellar with dreams of glamour ... only to end up disappointed by doing janitorial jobs. But it is a fact of life that some of the most important tasks at a winery are not done directly with the wine but rather with the physical facility and the tools of the trade.

SANITATION

For a winemaker who wants to be in control, the single most important cellar operation is keeping everything clean so contamination does not occur. This means cleaning equipment, tanks, barrels, walls, floors, ceilings, and anything else the wine or hose end may come into contact with. It's a thankless and ongoing job, but a dirty drain can mean the difference between success and failure—even when everything else has been done meticulously in the vineyard and cellar.

EQUIPMENT

Keeping equipment in top condition preserves wine quality and keeps cellar operations timely and dependable. Hose fittings that leak introduce unknown amounts of oxygen into the wine. Worn corker jaws that do not fit precisely can crease the cork and cause it to leak. Most cellar jobs are time-dependent and equipment breakdowns on filtering day or bottling day can be disastrous to the schedule.

WHAT'S NEXT FOR THE WINE?

Through the routine work of the cellar the developing wines begin to show their personalities. Some, such as a charming, fresh, young Beaujolais or Dolcetto d'Alba, are now ready for the world. Others must go on to "university," so to speak, to develop their full potential. This will come in the form of blending and extended aging, the next steps on the road to wine.

Cellar workers spend a lot of time doing down-and-dirty jobs such as "racking," during which wines are moved from one vessel to another to aerate, add oxygen, or move the wine off its sediments.

YOU CAN DO IT— YOURSELF

You don't have to own a vineyard or winery to make your own wine! In today's complex wine industry, it is possible to become involved in producing your own brand without the huge expense of planting vineyards and building a production facility. On a larger, commercial level it's not hard to find "virtual" wineries that contract grapes from established growers and then purchase winemaking services from wineries that do "custom crush" and contract winemaking.

On a smaller scale, perhaps for those who want to see firsthand what it's like to make wine before plunging in on a full-time basis, there are companies, such as Crushpad, located in Napa Valley, that have created a user-friendly blueprint for making small batches of wine. This is suited for people from wine enthusiasts to restaurateurs or retailers who wish to have a personal brand. Crushpad is an actual state-of-the art winery with a winemaking team and fruit from more than fifty vineyards. They even offer advice and instructions on turning a passion for wine into a business.

Finally, for the hobby wine enthusiast, there are winemaking facilities, such as the chic City Winery in New York City, that offer customers the chance to ferment, age, and bottle as little as a quarter barrel of their own wine—in a fun bar/restaurant-like atmosphere.

City Winery, located in Soho's Hudson Square, offers members the chance to make their own private-label wines. It also serves as a wine bar, gathering site, and private event space.

City Winery sells "barrel ownership," "barrel shares," and even "corporate barrel ownership." Members may participate in the winemaking process as little or as much as desired.

By making winemaking easily available to anyone, Crushpad "wants to liberate winemaking from the stereotype of the fifth-generation wine family living on a château with the Golden Retriever."

Crushpad focuses on making wine in small lots and aspires, as one customer said, "to make our wine fantasies come true."

Crushpad offers a "hands-on" winemaking experience for anyone with a serious interest in wine.

City Winery is designed for an individual, a couple, or a small group of friends who want to make their own barrel of wine. Customers can choose grapes from as far-flung places as Oregon, California, and Argentina.

Winemaker Rich Olsen-Harbich, right, and cellarmaster Don "Vino" Cavaluzzi, work together at Raphael winery, using sustainable vineyard practices, hand harvesting, spontaneous fermentation, and a natural winemaking philosophy.

INTERVIEW WITH:
RICHARD OLSEN-HARBICH AND DON "VINO" CAVALUZZI
RAPHAEL, PECONIC, NEW YORK, UNITED STATES

RICHARD OLSEN-HARBICH HAS BEEN WINEMAKER AT THE ABSOLUTELY ELEGANT RAPHAEL WINERY ON THE NORTH FORK OF LONG ISLAND, NEW YORK, SINCE IT WAS ESTABLISHED BY THE PETROCELLI FAMILY IN 1996.

Richard and I have known each other since he first started working on Long Island thirty-some years ago. When I spoke to him about his "natural winemaking philosophy" and how he handles routine jobs such as fining and filtering, he referred me to his cellarmaster, Don "Vino" Cavaluzzi, who has built a retirement hobby/second career working in the cellar at Rafael.

Don's background is not in winemaking. For thirty years, he and his wife owned and operated a printing and direct mail advertising business. Then, after five years of retirement, they started asking each other "now what do we do?" A new winery being built in Peconic, five miles from their home, provided the answer. Don has now been working in the cellar for nine years, and he proves that anybody can be a winemaker.

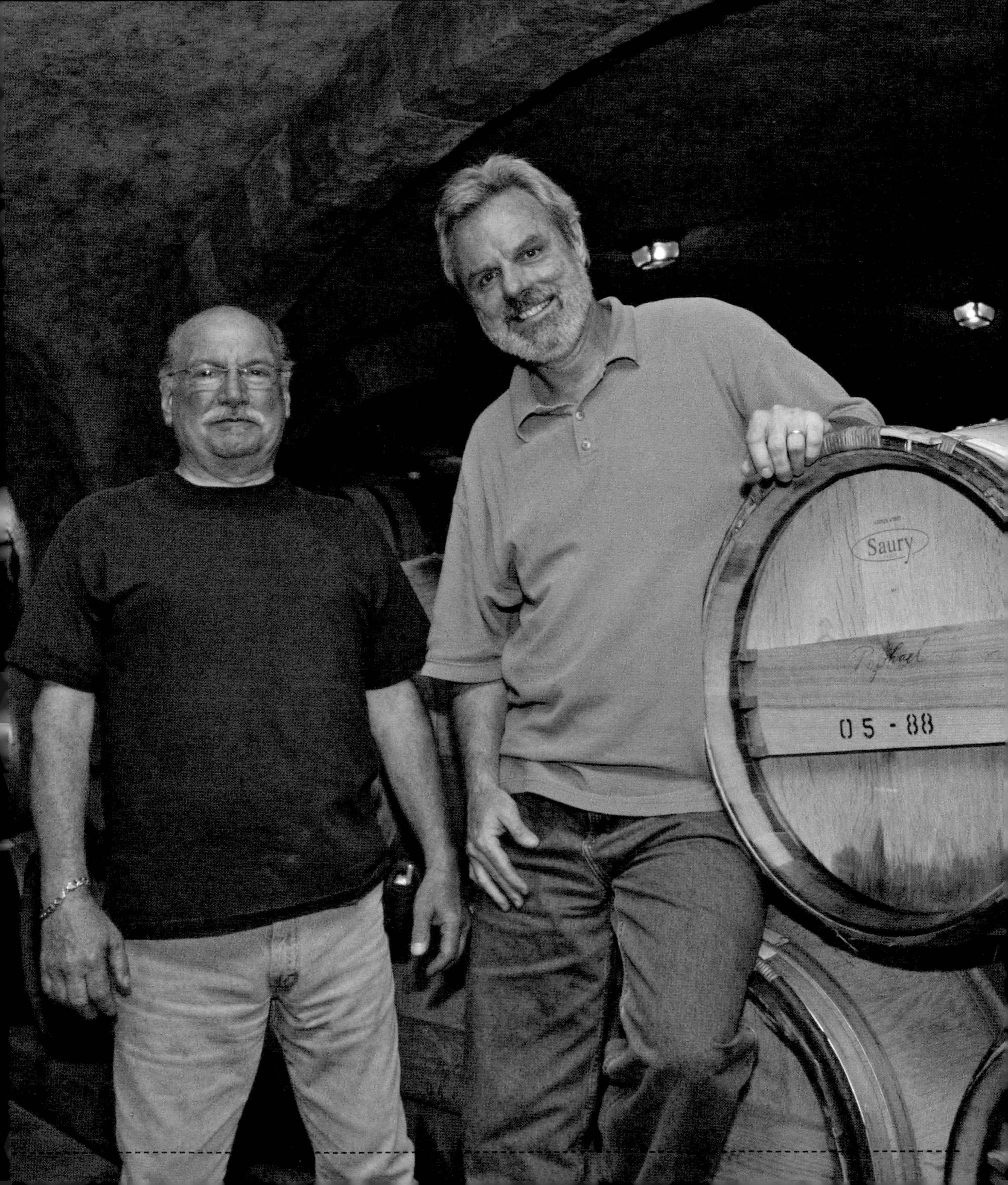
Saury
05 - 88

Raphael winery on the North Fork of Long Island, New York, perches its tanks on a flat sloping pad for ease of access and cleaning. Note the dimpled jackets through which a food-grade coolant is used to control temperatures.

DON, I UNDERSTAND YOU ARE THE CELLARMASTER AT RAPHAEL. PLEASE TELL ME A LITTLE ABOUT IT.

Cellarmaster, assistant to the winemaker, whatever you want to call me. What I do is take care of the cellar, the mechanics of the cellar. I don't really get involved with the hands-on winemaking decisions. It's not my thing. That's Rich's thing.

I KNOW THAT EVERYTHING ABOUT RAFAEL IS DELIBERATE, COMPLETELY THOUGHT OUT, AND PERFECTLY EXECUTED … AND THAT RICH WOULD NOT ENTRUST HIS WINES TO ANYONE NOT COMMITTED TO HIS VISION.

Rich and I get along very well. We get the job done. I take care of the equipment. I keep it clean. This is what I do, and I love it. I really love it. And I've learned a lot. This was supposed to be a one- or two-day-a-week job, but now I'm working six days—I don't know what happened!

HOW DID IT HAPPEN?

I started out picking grapes, just to get out of the house. That's when I met Rich, and he was frustrated because it was harvest time and one of his young college guys was leaving early. He asked if I was interested in the job. Actually, he asked if I thought I could handle the job. I figured after thirty years of running a business I could handle anything. That's how I got started here, and I'm completely enjoying it.

LET'S TALK ABOUT THE CELLAR AND WHAT YOU DO. WHAT ARE THE IMPORTANT THINGS YOU DO TO MAKE GOOD WINE?

I feel the most important thing is to keep the equipment clean. I've been in some wineries in which you have to roll your pant cuffs up when you walk through. Not at our place. I've had some tours come here from local hospitals, and I have heard comments like "This place is cleaner than some of our ORs!"

And, obviously, I do what Rich says, when he says it. I keep the pumps and hoses working. If pieces have to be added to the bottling line, or moved, that's what I do. Or when we're filtering, I set up and operate the filter. And then I break it down and clean it. I take every pad out and then I take every screen out and scrub them. When I hear that some people don't clean their filters, it makes my hair stand up (what little hair I have left).

I CAN SEE YOU'RE BIG ON CLEANING.

It's in my background, from the printing world. If you want a perfect color on the press, you have to have a clean press to start with. It's the same with wine. It's got to be clean.

The John Petrocelli family, owners of Raphael winery, "strives to produce Long Island's greatest wines, incorporating both New World advances and Old World traditions." Raphael produces handcrafted wines that reflect the unique climate and soil of the North Fork of Long Island.

A cellar worker uses this stainless steel device
to stir the "lees"—yeast sediments left over
from fermentation—in each barrel to extract
flavors and textures during the aging process.

WHAT DO YOU USE FOR CLEANING?

We keep our chemicals at a minimum; everything we use is natural, and that's extremely important in winemaking as far as I'm concerned. For cleaning the bottling line we have one-inch lines that pump 175°F (79.4°C) water at very high pressure. For cleaning the tanks we use basic soda ash, and then rinse with hot water. And then we neutralize it with citric and sulfite.

When our barrels are empty, we wash them out with hot water running through a spinning spray head. When this takes off in the barrel, it spins so loud it sounds like a B29 landing! Then we burn a sulfur tablet inside to keep any bacteria from growing.

WHAT WOULD YOU TELL SOMEONE WHO IS THINKING OF CHANGING CAREERS AND GOING INTO WINEMAKING?

I'd probably retreat to that old adage that says "If you want to make a small fortune in the wine business, you have to start off with a large fortune."

Really, I'd tell them I like the mechanical end of it. I like dealing with equipment. And if they want to get involved, they can't be afraid to get their hands dirty. You'd have to ask Rich about the actual winemaking part.

RICH, I'VE BEEN TALKING TO DON ABOUT THE WORK OF THE CELLAR, AFTER THE WINES ARE FERMENTED AND BEFORE THEY'RE FINISHED AND SENT TO THE BOTTLING LINE. FROM YOUR PERSPECTIVE, WHAT ARE THE MOST IMPORTANT THINGS THAT YOU DO?

Monitoring! At this stage of the game I'm constantly checking to see how the wines are progressing. I'm taking temperatures, maybe twice a week, to see if the (sugar) fermentations are all wrapped up. I use only native yeast, so the fermentations can drag on for quite a while. And the reds may be going through their malolactic fermentation, so I'm watching that as well.

And I'm being very vigilant that all the tanks are full, topped up. I'm kind of a reductive, anti-oxygen winemaker, so I'm trying to keep things away from air as much as possible, right from the get-go. When I feel that a wine is done, when it has nowhere else to go, then I'll sulfite and rack.

DO YOU LET ANY OF THE WHITES OR REDS SIT WITH THE BIOMASS (YEAST HULLS, LEES, SEDIMENTS)?

Sometimes—if it's tasting well and it's not getting too reductive and there aren't any funky flavors coming in. But sometimes with the whites, especially, I'm actually looking for some of that funk.

I LOVE THAT WORD! BUT HOW DO YOU DEFINE "FUNK"? WHAT'S A GOOD FUNK, OR A BAD FUNK?

We're talking about hedonistic observations here … but to me, a bad funk, especially in whites, is when there's a hydrogen sulfide, reductive type of smell. It can eventually form mercaptan and ethyl mercaptan (sulfur-related smells often described as "rotten eggs"), something that is very difficult to get rid of.

In reds, the funk is sometimes sweet and pungent. Sweaty. Sometimes an animal, "barnyard" smell. Cellar smells. In the industry we often say "earthy." That sounds better than sweaty or animal.

WHAT DO YOU RELATE THESE FUNKY SMELLS TO?

These smells might be related to the indigenous yeast, or the indigenous ML. If I have a lot that is finishing ML and I see that, I don't freak out. One of the funny things about wine is that I'm often looking for that kind of complexity—a little earthiness. So that can become a "good funk." But if I see hydrogen sulfide starting to rear its head, then I'll typically do a racking right away.

HOW ABOUT FINING AND FILTERING?

I'm not much into fining and filtration. Typically if I do it, it is mostly on the whites. I'll do a bentonite fining right at pressing, and then one or possibly two filtrations. Quite often we'll get by with just one. On the reds, I'm not filtering at all. I'm trying to let them settle naturally, and then they will go through a flycatcher type of cartridge filter at the bottling line, just to grab anything that might be visible.

I will do an egg white fining on the reds if they need it. We get fresh eggs right from a farmer close by, and we do it quickly, in the barrel, for forty, forty-five days. It's a very gentle way of fining. I've tried other things in the past, such as gelatin and casein, but I just got to the point where I felt like I wasn't being sincere to the wine; I really wanted to trust what the wine was rather than trying to change it. So in the past five or six years I've gone to pretty much nothing.

THAT "NATURAL" APPROACH PRETTY MUCH DEFINES YOUR WHOLE PHILOSOPHY OF WINEMAKING, DOESN'T IT?

Yes. I've stopped playing with things. I think in the past we've paid too much attention to acid and pH levels, sulfites and stability, rather than just looking at the wine as a whole. How it tastes. When I do something "unnatural" to a wine it always sticks out. I can see it. I can feel it. The public doesn't know it, but I know it.

I trust what the wine wants to do and I try to be really vigilant from the first day that fruit comes in, even before that, in the vineyard. That's where the job gets done. Once we get to the cellar, we just try to prevent things from happening.

"In the past we've paid too much attention to acid and pH levels, sulfites and stability, rather than just looking at the wine as a whole. How it tastes. When I do something 'unnatural' to a wine it always sticks out. I can see it. I can feel it. The public doesn't know it, but I know it."

I CAN SEE WINEMAKING IS VERY PERSONAL TO YOU, AND LOCAL. I LOVE THAT ATTITUDE. YOUR WINES HAVE A SIGNATURE FLAVOR.

They're quite well structured and complex. I don't want to make just "mainstream" wines. I feel that we are making the wines engendered by Long Island's terroir.

YOU ARE SO WELL KNOWN AS A LEADER IN ESTABLISHING REGIONAL IDENTITY AND VINIFICATION TECHNIQUES FOR LONG ISLAND. I'VE REALLY ENJOYED HEARING ABOUT THE RAPHAEL CELLAR FROM BOTH YOUR PERSPECTIVE AND DON'S.

We're a pretty good team. I've set a theme that's about natural fermentation and a natural winemaking style. And Don makes sure we're carrying out that program and getting everything done right.

Among hardworking cellar rats at the end of an exhausting week, the favorite slogan is "It takes a lot of beer to make great wine!"

AS I WAS GROWING UP, MY MOTHER WAS A WELL-APPRECIATED COOK WHO BECAME A GREAT CHEF. SHE WAS FROM OKLAHOMA AND I CAN STILL REMEMBER HER FRIED CHICKEN, CHICKEN FRIED STEAK, FRIED ANYTHING. WE WOULD HAVE EATEN HER CHICKEN AND DUMPLINGS EVERY NIGHT. I TRY NOT TO THINK ABOUT HER VEGETABLES BECAUSE THEY MOSTLY CAME OUT OF CANS, AND EVERYTHING—FROM CARROTS TO ASPARAGUS—HAD THE CONSISTENCY OF MASHED POTATOES. THIS WAS GOOD PREPARATION FOR THE NEXT CULINARY STAGE OF MY LIFE WHEN MY FATHER MOVED THE FAMILY TO ENGLAND AND I WAS SENT TO BRITISH BOARDING SCHOOL.

CHAPTER 9:
CREATING BLENDS

The great winemakers of Bordeaux have honed their craft over centuries, truly exemplifying "Old World" winemaking traditions.

But something had happened by the time I arrived home on my first school break. My folks now had a French chef and housekeeper who served snails from the fallen-down barn behind the house and crème brûlée for dessert. I was not always enamored with the food choices, but suddenly things had flavor, lots of flavor! It got even better the next year when we moved to Paris and Julia Child signed mom up at her Trois Gourmandes cooking school— suddenly I was living in a world of herbs and spices, aromas and textures, sauces that elevated a slice of meat to a religious experience and made everything on the plate more exciting.

Chaddsford Winery cellarmaster Jim Osborn and winemaker Eric Miller do about half their tasting in the lab because it is a neutral zone with limited smells, good lighting, and tools for blending trials.

I don't think I fully understood the majesty and imaginative complexity of gourmet cuisine until I became a winemaker and delved into the fine art of blending.

DEFINING BLENDS IN WINEMAKING

Blending wine in the cellar is simply putting pieces together—in this case, different grape varieties or wines—to make a better whole. It is the obscure crossover of science and art. It is where logical thinking, technical understanding, and experience intersect with abilities and sensitivities that can't be taught. It is when a finished wine becomes an entity greater than its original parts.

Blending is done for many reasons that range from legacy and legality to consistency and economy to the health of the wine itself. Furthermore, there are several different types of blends, including field blends, varietal blends, and cross-vintage blends.

FIELD BLENDS

At one time, probably all wines were blends of grape varieties grown in the same vineyard or vineyard rows, then picked, carried in, processed, and fermented as single lots that were bottled and consumed by the farmers who grew them. Today, most vineyards have gone to monoculture, growing each variety in its most favorable site, and most wineries process each variety from each vineyard separately. And recently we have seen the emergence of "terroir" blends that emphasize and rely on the harmony of the site, soil, and climate of the vineyard by merging all of the grapes grown on the site into a single cuvée.

VARIETAL BLENDS

Different varieties of grapes are often mixed together in blends to emphasize the best qualities of each, to improve or enhance certain characteristics, or to create something unique or unusual. Certain areas have long histories and are known for blending an exclusive group of varieties, such as Bordeaux, where primarily Cabernet Sauvignon, Merlot, and Cabernet Franc are used. A New World category of wine, "GSM" (named after the varieties Grenache, Syrah, and Mourvèdre), has been developed to emulate the kind of blending done in France's Châteauneuf-du-Pape region.

CROSS-VINTAGE BLENDS

Many wines bear a vintage date on the label (always referring to the year the grapes were grown); others may be blends of different vintage years. This may happen to maintain consistency when the winemaker is more concerned with style than showcasing the characteristics of a single growing season, or it may happen because of economic need or necessity, as when the winery has too much of a single variety to sell from a single vintage. Such overflows may end up in a "dumping pot" that is not unusual to find in small winery cellars.

WHY BLEND?

Some blends are determined by tradition, legalities, or a combination of both. In Priorato, Spain, for example, it is hard to find a red wine that does not blend some Garnacha (Grenache) and some Cariñena (Carignan). Very few people can name all the grapes traditionally used in Chianti, but we all know what that familiar blend tastes like!

Other times, blends are done for consistency and economy. While a small family winery might take pride in how their wines differ to reflect each vintage, larger wineries that sell wine worldwide look for consistency not only from bottle to bottle but also from year to year. A classic success story is Gallo's Hearty Burgundy, sourced from far-reaching vineyards, made from several varieties, available in gallon jugs, never vintage-dated, inexpensive, and known to satisfy many a critic in blind tastings.

Sometimes winemakers blend varieties simply to take advantage of or to use up available materials, such as a few barrels or lots that are just too small to bottle separately.

Blending may be done for balance, as when a lot is too sweet, or too dry, or too soft, or too acidic. Young wines with pH levels in the "danger zone" (above 4.0 pH) are frequently blended with a higher acid wine. It might be done to create a style of watery freshness by blending for low alcohol. It could be the old iron fist of mouth-drying tannins in a velvet glove of soft, low acid. The desired balance for a high-acid white might be softened just so by blending in a sweeter wine.

In some cases, blending is one of the last options for covering up serious flaws such as browning of the wine or highly flavored bacterial infections. Successful blending in this situation can be very difficult to achieve because overcoming or dominating a small amount of some "off" characteristic may require an inordinate amount of good-quality material.

Finally, we must not forget the winemaker's artistic side! Like music, like painting, like other art forms, some blends are created just to express individual creativity or vision, or to enhance complexity and make a wine more interesting. Tannins, color, acidity, fruit, sweetness, earthiness, smoke—all become instruments in the composer's symphony. Also on the artist's palette are experience, restraint, instinct, subtlety, depth, and personal preference. Is it any wonder there are so many different wines of so many different styles being made around the world?

Knowing how brief their tenure has been compared to Old World regions, even third-generation New World winemakers do extensive analysis, trials, and tastings before making final blending decisions.

When a large lot is assembled from many small barrels, every single barrel must be tasted and assessed for quality and its effect on the finished blend.

HOW BLENDS ARE MADE

Some blends are conceived when the winemaker sees and tastes the grapes while they are still hanging on the vine. Some are conceptualized while walking through the cellar tasting various cuveés. But all come to life in the laboratory.

Prior to the physical act of blending, each component being considered is studied and tasted. Samples are taken from each separate tank or barrel and bench trials (sample blends) are set up in a neutral—almost clinical—tasting area. The blends and control wines are then tasted by the winemaker, enologist, and selected members of the winemaking team. This is where the discipline of spitting, versus drinking, maintains a clear mind and separates amateurs from professionals!

Ideally, measuring cylinders and a good supply of each wine being considered are on hand for last-minute blending—plus a lot of glassware for informal glass-to-glass pouring as new options are discussed and considered.

Before the final decisions are made, each wine's analysis and history is reviewed, because it will become a part of the new formula that is ultimately selected. When a determination is made, the actual components out in the cellar are gently and thoroughly mixed—and begin their new life as a wedded entity.

It is the winemaker's goal to make blends as many months as possible after fermentation so the components are in a near-typical state. Conversely, blends are done as long before bottling as possible so the resulting wine can be tasted, tested, and possibly touched up before the aging program is over.

Many winemakers have their barrels custom made with particular wines or blends in mind. The story of this French oak barrel can be seen in the detailed information stamped on the head, indicating things such as (FO) French oak, (FB) forest blend (vs. a particular forest such as Nevers or Allier), (H) heavy toast, (TH) toasted head, (2Y) 2 year air-dried.

WORLDWIDE BLENDS

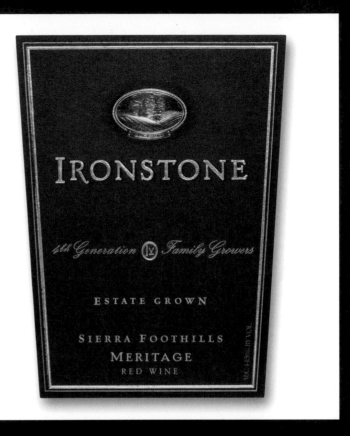

VARIETAL BLENDS
Multiple-grape blends such as this California Meritage show complexity because of the melding of different varieties. Meritage is a (registered) proprietary term used to denote red and white Bordeaux-style wines using the same grapes as their famous Old World counterparts.

TRADITIONAL BLENDS
The blending regulations in Chianti, Italy, have evolved over the past two hundred years to today's requirement for a minimum of 80 percent Sangiovese plus the likes of Canaiolo, Trebbiano, Syrah, and Cabernet Sauvignon.

TERROIR (FIELD) BLENDS
The natural harmony of several grape varieties grown on the same site has been known for hundreds of years but is most unusual in this complex blend from the Miller Estate Vineyard, which incorporates all red grapes grown on the site.

INTERVIEW WITH:
PAULINE VAUTHIER
CHÂTEAU AUSONE, BORDEAUX, FRANCE

WHEN MY GOOD FRIEND CARL PETRILLO, AN AVOWED BORDEAUX LOVER WITH A BRILLIANT WINE CELLAR, INVITED ME TO JOIN HIM ON A JUNKET TO SOME OF OUR FAVORITE CHÂTEAUX, ONE OF THE HIGHLIGHTS WAS A VISIT TO CHÂTEAU AUSONE. THAT DAY, DURING THE REST OF OUR BORDEAUX EXPLORATION, AND FOR MANY YEARS AFTERWARD, WE RECALLED WITH AWE THE REMARKABLE EXPERIENCE OF TOURING WITH THE WINEMAKER AND TASTING SEVERAL VINTAGES OF THIS PRIZED AND RARE JEWEL. AT THE TIME, WE DIDN'T REALIZE WE WERE ARRIVING JUST AS A REGIME CHANGE WAS ABOUT TO TAKE THIS VENERABLE HOUSE TO EVEN GREATER HEIGHTS.

To fully understand stately, dignified, respected Bordeaux châteaux such as Ausone, one must look at the history and long experience such properties are steeped in. It is likely that the high ground around the town of Saint-Émilion, including Château Ausone, was first planted around the year 300 C.E. In addition to the profound insights gleaned over nearly two thousand years, Château Ausone has been in the hands of the same family since 1718. In the late 1800s it was held in highest esteem and was consequently ranked as Premier Grand Cru Classé (A) in the official 1955 Classification of Saint-Émilion—one of only two châteaux in Saint-Émilion to be granted that distinction.

In the mid-1990s Alain Vauthier took over as managing director of all three of his family's properties: Château Moulin Saint Georges, Château de Fonbel, and Château Ausone. Later, he installed his daughter, Pauline, to oversee the vineyards and winemaking at all three properties. Mademoiselle Vauthier was well prepared to take the reins as a result of her enology and viticulture studies at Lycée Agroviticole de Libourne-Montagne and a stint working in South Africa as assistant cellarmaster (*maître de chais*).

When I contacted Pauline Vauthier, my interest was to better understand the unique wines of Ausone by discovering the blending decisions behind them.

Pauline Vauthier, winemaker and scion of the family that owns and operates Château Ausone, Château Moulin Saint Georges, and Château de Fonbel, all in the commune of Saint-Émilion.

PAULINE, TELL ME ABOUT YOUR ROLE AT CHÂTEAU AUSONE.

I have been working at Ausone since 2005. I work with my father; as you know, this is a family business. I'm in charge of all the vinification and aging of the wines, and also the vineyards. Château Ausone has vineyards of 7 hectares (18 acres) and we produce just two thousand cases of wine each vintage.

WHAT ABOUT YOUR OTHER FAMILY PROPERTIES?

I also work at our other properties. In total we manage 80 hectares (198 acres) of vines, all of them in St.-Émilion, all with the St.-Émilion appellation.

THAT'S A LOT FOR BORDEAUX, ISN'T IT?

Yes, but I'm very glad that all the vineyards are in St.-Émilion. It's fortunate because I don't have to travel so far and it's a lot easier to keep track of the weather in such a small area.

WHEN I VISITED CHÂTEAU AUSONE (IN 1995), PASCAL DELBECK WAS IN CHARGE OF THE CELLARS. HOW HAVE THE WINES CHANGED SINCE YOU BEGAN TO MAKE THEM?

There was a big change at Ausone in 2000 when my father alone became responsible for making the wine. We began to make changes in the vineyard. We started to do a green harvest, de-leafing, working the vines like a small garden. And we also began to work very differently in the cellar. We changed to a very small, light extraction, so not a lot of pump-over or *délestage* (separating the juice from the seeds). We moved to small wood tanks and began to use 100 percent new barrels for each vintage. But we don't want to have too much wood—the taste of too much wood in the wine—so we use a light toast on the barrels. We wanted to age the wine, but not to make the wine taste like wood!

WHAT I'M REALLY CURIOUS ABOUT IS THE BLENDING AT CHÂTEAU AUSONE. WHAT IS THE BLEND YOU USE?

There are just two varieties we use for Château Ausone: Merlot and Cabernet Franc. In St.-Émilion the most important grape is Merlot, but at Ausone, the majority is Cabernet Franc, about 55 percent.

Our terroir is very well adapted to this variety. Our soil is a mixture of clay on limestone. Also, our vineyards are elevated, facing south on steep slopes, so we have very good sun exposure, which is good for maturing and ripening the fruit. In St.-Émilion, on the Right Bank, it is hard to grow and ripen Cabernet Sauvignon as they do on the Left Bank—that is the reason we have a lot of Cabernet Franc. When I arrived we decided to plant even more, so I hope in five or ten years we can increase the blend to 60 or 65 percent Cabernet Franc in the Grand Vin. Right now these young vines are going into our second wine, Chapelle d'Ausone.

Château Ausone on the Right Bank of Bordeaux, is classified among the top growths of Bordeaux and is the rarest due to its tiny annual production of just two thousand cases of wine.

SO YOU ARE PLANNING TO INCREASE THE BLEND FROM 55 PERCENT CABERNET FRANC TO 60 OR 65 PERCENT?

We will see! But no more than that, because we want to keep Merlot in the blend. If we went to 100 percent Cabernet Franc, the wine would be too tannic, not velvety. The Merlot gives a lot of softness and we want to keep a little bit of that.

THAT'S INTERESTING. SO YOU FEEL YOUR CABERNET FRANC, BESIDES ITS GOOD CHARACTERISTICS, HAS TOO MUCH TANNIN, IT'S TOO HARD? IT'S ALMOST LIKE CABERNET SAUVIGNON OVER ON THE LEFT BANK OF BORDEAUX, IN MÉDOC?

Well, as I said, we don't use Cabernet Sauvignon here on the Right Bank. But I see what you are saying—our Cabernet Franc in the Right Bank plays the same role in the blend as Cabernet Sauvignon does in the Left Bank, to make the wine hard and firm. And Merlot softens it. At one time, historically, Cabernet was the majority in all of France, but after the phylloxera crisis [see sidebar], when the vineyards were replanted all the winemakers planted Merlot. Merlot is easier to cultivate, and the Merlot produces more.

Most of the vineyards in France were replanted after the devastating phylloxera epidemic in the late nineteenth century, when a root louse native to North America was introduced to the vineyards of Europe. It is estimated that between two-thirds and nine-tenths of all European vineyards were destroyed by phylloxera, microscopic pests that feed on the roots and leaves of grape vines.

The rustic cellars of Château Ausone were carved out of limestone; much of the nearby town of Saint-Émilion was built with the same stone.

WHAT OTHER FEATURES DO YOU LIKE IN MERLOT?

I love the softness and the gentle tannins. In Ausone, the Cabernet Franc provides the full body and the structure and minerality. But if you don't add Merlot, the wine will be too austere.

TELL ME ABOUT THE VINTAGE-SPECIFIC ISSUES THAT CONCERN YOU WHEN YOU BLEND FOR CHÂTEAU AUSONE.

My main concern is that every vintage blend is similar, within about 5 percent. The Cabernet Franc could be 45 percent or 50 percent or 55 percent, as long as it's not unique or different for just one vintage. I prefer for it to be always of consistent flavor, texture, color, and longevity. Ausone lives a very long time.

HOW DO YOU WORK UP TO THAT FINAL BLEND? DO YOU JUST KNOW IT INTUITIVELY, OR DO YOU DO IT BY TASTE?

It involves a lot of things, not always the same. If you take our current vintage as an example, I knew during vinification as I tasted each tank to see which were very good. When I bought barrels I decided which parts were going into the Château Ausone blend, and which were going into the second wine.

DO YOU USE LABORATORY TESTS TO HELP MAKE YOUR DECISIONS?

To determine the final blend, I work with my father and my cellarmaster. We have all the barrels, we taste, and we make the mix. We try it and we decide. There is no laboratory.

I'M SURPRISED. AT MY WINERY WE DO ANALYSIS OF EVERY LOT. WE KNOW THE pH, WE KNOW THE TA (TOTAL ACIDITY), WE KNOW EVERYTHING.

It was like that when I worked in South Africa before coming to Ausone. All the time, all those samples, measuring the pH and the alcohols—we did all of that, but we didn't taste the berries—and for me that was very strange. So if the analysis was good, we would begin the harvest but without tasting the berries! At Château Ausone, the most important thing is to taste. We have no lab in the château! Nearby, yes, but just for a few analyses such as pH.

I GUESS YOU HAVE A LOT OF HISTORY TO GO ON, A LONG RECORD OF WORKING WITH JUST THIS ONE SITE, JUST TWO GRAPE VARIETIES, MAKING JUST THIS ONE INCREDIBLE WINE. IT'S VERY DIFFERENT FROM WHAT IS DONE IN LARGE NEW WORLD WINERIES, WHERE WE MAY BE WORKING WITH TEN OR TWENTY VINEYARDS AND THAT MANY GRAPE VARIETIES. IS THERE ANYTHING ELSE THAT PLAYS INTO YOUR DECISION, ANY CHARACTERISTICS YOU FEEL A WINEMAKER SHOULD HAVE TO MAKE A GOOD BLEND?

A winemaker must have a feeling, an imagination. Maybe a mix of feeling and imagination so that when you taste you can imagine what you can make. And experience. In my opinion, if you taste a lot, you learn to taste better. When I began, it was very difficult for me. And now, it's not easy but easier. So practice, practice, practice. Sometimes we will taste one hundred wines in a day.

Château Ausone remains uncompromised by bottling a second label, Chapelle d'Ausone, using younger vines and barrels that do not make the first cut.

WHEN DO YOU FINISH THE BLENDING OF YOUR WINES?

We must complete the blends in April because in Bordeaux we have the traditional Tasting en Primeur the first week in April and we have to present the final blend. This is when all of our clients in the trade and the media come to Bordeaux to taste the new vintage and to decide what they are going to buy. It is a tradition that is very important to us in Bordeaux.

These experts come and taste, and they give us their opinions about the wine, and after this we put a price on the wine and they buy it, as futures. But the wine will not be bottled until next July, over a year later, and delivered the following February. So they pay for the wine well before the bottling and delivery, based just on the blend and how it tastes.

THAT'S A GREAT BUSINESS. MOST WINERIES AROUND THE WORLD WISH THEY COULD BE PAID FOR THEIR WINES TWO YEARS BEFORE DELIVERY!

It's a very old system in Bordeaux. It's been like that for thirty or forty years. Everything is old in Bordeaux!

"A winemaker must have a feeling, an imagination. Maybe a mix of feeling and imagination so that when you taste you can imagine what you can make."

AFTER YOU MAKE YOUR BLENDS FOR THE TASTING EN PRIMEUR, DO YOU EVER GO BACK AND MAKE ADJUSTMENTS AFTERWARD?

Sometimes it changes a little bit, but the maximum is 5 percent change—we are required to present the final blend during the tasting. The client wants to make sure the product he receives in the bottle is the same as what he tasted. This year, the vintage is very good, so I'm sure that the blend will not change.

DO YOU HAVE ANY OTHER THOUGHTS YOU WANT TO SHARE ON BLENDING? DOES IT BECOME AUTOMATIC FOR YOU, OR DO YOU STILL WORRY ABOUT WHETHER YOU'VE MADE THE RIGHT BLEND?

The blending is very important—with the blending you make the wine. The final wine. The feeling of the wine. When we make the blends, we are very happy because we have made the best possible mix that we will present at the Tasting en Primeur. But we are also very anxious, because we are thinking, is it the right percentage, not too much Merlot, not too much Cabernet Franc? Will they recognize the good quality? So we will ask questions about the blends and wonder until after the Tasting en Primeur. And then when other people taste it and when we have heard very good commentary, then we can relax—only then.

ONE LAST QUESTION: HAVE YOU EVER HAD A DISASTER AND MADE A WRONG BLEND?

No. I cross my fingers. Never!

Château Ausone grows a high percentage of Cabernet Franc vines because so much of its 7-hectare (18 acre) vineyard is on a deep, cracked bed of limestone.

FIRST GROWTH, SECOND GROWTH, PREMIER CRU … WHAT?

In 1855, Emperor Napoleon III asked brokers from the wine industry to create a classification system that would rank France's best Bordeaux wines according to their reputation and trading price—which at the time was directly related to quality. In what we have come to know as the "Bordeaux Wine Official Classification of 1855," the significant red wines were ranked in importance from first to fifth growths, or *crus*. (The whites, considered much less important, were ranked only from first growth to second growth.) Within each category, the various châteaux were ranked in order of quality, and only twice since then has there been a change, in 1856 and 1973.

At the top of the list, the First Growths, or Premiers Crus, are just five hallowed names that are eminently recognizable around the world: Château Lafite Rothschild, Château Latour, Château Margaux, Château Haut-Brion, and Château Mouton Rothschild (reclassified from Second Growth status in 1973). All of these are from the Médoc, except Haut-Brion, which is from Graves.

Since 1855, many of the ranked properties have expanded, shrunk, and/or been divided. Vineyards have changed hands and some châteaux are now recognized as far exceeding earlier, more modest classifications. Numerous wine critics have argued that these rankings have become outdated and do not provide an accurate guide to the quality of the wines being made on each estate today.

Showcasing further just how different the traditional "Old World" is from the "New World" of winemaking, Bordeaux is also home to other classification systems, including the 1955 Classification of Saint-Émilion wines, a list that is updated every ten years or so.

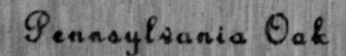

Keystone Cooperage

Pennsylvania Oak

M+

TH

2Y

AFTER FERMENTATION, FINING, FILTERING, AND/OR A PERIOD OF COMING TOGETHER, SOME WINES ARE BASICALLY "DONE" AND READY TO MOVE INTO BOTTLES FOR SALE AS LIGHT, FRESH WINES—MOST OFTEN WHITES OR ROSÉS—TO BE ENJOYED FOR THE EXUBERANCE OF THEIR YOUTH. THESE WINES (AMONG MY FAVORITES ARE THE YOUNG VINHO VERDES OF PORTUGAL) WILL TYPICALLY SPEND THEIR LIFE IN NEUTRAL CONTAINERS, SUCH AS STAINLESS STEEL OR GLASS-LINED TANKS, AND WILL BE CONSUMED WITHIN TWO OR THREE YEARS OF THEIR VINTAGE DATE.

CHAPTER 10:
BARREL AGING

At the end of the process, the barrel's pedigree is branded on the head. This particular finished product from well-respected custom barrel maker Keystone Cooperage of Pennsylvania (United States) tells this story: Pennsylvania-grown oak, medium-plus toast with a toasted head, and staves that were air-dried for two years.

Other wines—primarily reds—are not quite finished and will move into an extended period of aging and maturing. This next phase typically takes place in wooden barrels post-fermentation and before bottling. It ranges from a couple of months to a couple of years. Like blending, decisions about barrel aging allow the winemaker to create a personal style and put a unique "stamp" on the developing wines.

In some cases, the process of aging adds longevity to a wine, but in all cases it adds complexity. In the course of aging wine, some things are added, some are taken away, some are intensified, some are compounded in new ways, and some are simply maintained. Tasting the evolution of a wine during aging is a long, slow thriller as wines begin to develop and show real grace, charm, and power.

WHAT HAPPENS DURING BARREL AGING?

Barrel aging begins when a wine is finished fermenting and is moved into an oak barrel or larger wood container. It is generally believed that the wine's life is extended, at least in part, due to the antioxidative effect of tannins absorbed into the wine as it sits in contact with the wood. Thus, tannins are often referred to as "natural preservatives" that allow certain wines to continue aging and maturing, even after they are bottled. At the same time these harsh, dry extracts and textures are being contributed, the wine will also pick up a toasty/smoky character from the interior of a barrel that has been glazed or toasted by the open flame used to soften and bend the staves.

Further, as a wine sits in the barrel, depending on the humidity of the cellar, a certain amount of liquid volume will evaporate and condense the wine, bringing delicate smells and flavors to the threshold of perception. Likewise, because wood is semipermeable, a tiny amount of oxygen penetrates the staves and barrelhead at just the right rate to allow oxidative reactions to occur (oxidation). Thus, harsh tannins are softened and color is stabilized. Some smells are enhanced or increased while others are reduced.

Finally, most wines prepared for aging are still cloudy and have some amount of healthy sediments (biomass or lees) that came from the grape and fermentation-related organisms. When the wine sits in contact with these sediments, it picks up desirable flavors and textures that are often described as "silkiness" or "body."

FACTORS THAT AFFECT BARREL AGING

THE SIZE AND SHAPE OF THE BARREL

A barrel's size and shape determine the amount of surface area the wine will be in contact with. The smaller the barrel, the more contact with the liquid and the more effect on the wine. The thickness of the barrel staves also plays a part in determining how much oxygen contact will occur. Large wooden vats that hold hundreds or thousands of gallons provide less surface for oxygen penetration than small barrels of around 60 gallons (227 L).

THE AGE OF THE BARREL

All wooden containers allow evaporation, concentration, and micro-oxidation, but older barrels yield diminishing volumes of flavors and preserving tannins over their first three to five years of service. Thus a winemaker must know the effect he or she is looking for in the finished wine before choosing whether to use a new barrel (which would contribute heavily) or an older barrel (with lesser contribution). In many cases, the decision may be to use some new oak and some older oak, blending the lots back together before bottling.

One big challenge of using old barrels is maintaining them. If they are left to sit empty in low humidity for more than sixty days they begin to dry out and leak. Thus a typical maintenance program might be rinsing with 150°F (65.6°C) water, followed by filling and soaking with a solution of sulfur dioxide and citric acid for two or three days, followed by draining for three days, followed by burning a sulfur wick and sealing to hold a sulfurous atmosphere for sixty days (to destroy any microorganisms lodged in the interior surface of the wood).

WHERE THE OAK IS GROWN

Where the oak is grown and its species affect the porosity of the wood and the characteristics that can be extracted from the barrel. American oak, for instance, is valued for its very forward characteristics that often show up as "spice" in Australian Shiraz and a "coconut" characteristic in some Chardonnays. Oak grown in the Nevers Forest of central France is prized for its subtle, almost sweet, vanilla-like taste. Hungarian oak, grown in the Tokai region, is becoming recognized for its subtle mix of sweet vanillans, firm tannins, and almost sappy raw oak/wood sensations.

HOW THE BARREL IS MADE

All barrels are made from the best cuts of furniture-quality wood. Air-dried oak is aged for months or years and is considered by many winemakers to be superior to kiln-dried staves, dried in a matter of days. Staves are heated, softened, and bent by steam, water or an open flame that provides a multitude of toasty, smoky flavor effects. Winemakers have many other choices to make when ordering custom-made barrels: Do the barrels have a light toast? Medium

toast? Or heavy toast? Are the ends, or heads, toasted as well as the staves? Each decision will be reflected in the overall characteristics of the finished wine.

HOW LONG DO WINES STAY IN BARREL?

How long a wine is in barrel is determined by when the desired effect is achieved, the style of wine being made, or when it tastes the way the winemaker has envisioned it. In short, delicate wines might do well

with minimal time in new flavorful barrels. Intensely dry tannic wines may need a year or two to soften and fully develop. It is one of the winemaker's great pleasures and responsibilities to evaluate each wine over the course of aging and to make the call. For the recently initiated winemaker, a new wine region, or new grape varieties, this double-edged pleasure becomes an agony of decision making that ensures that every wine in every cellar is unique.

Wood chips are considered to be an "oak derivative" because they can simulate the effect of traditional oak aging in barrels—in a much shorter period and at a substantially reduced cost.

ECONOMIC CONSIDERATIONS OF BARREL AGING

Barrel-aged wines are not necessarily better than light, fresh wines that never come in contact with wood, but they definitely cost more to make. The cost of a finely coopered barrel may be as much or more as the grapes that go into it. There is also the consideration of additional labor: whether a cuvée is made up of ten 60-gallon (227 L) barrels or one 600-gallon (2,271 L) tank, each container must be monitored, tested, tasted, tracked, and eventually transferred—which means ten times more labor if the wine is in small barrels.

These additional costs get passed on to the consumer, assuring that barrel-aged wines are more expensive than their light, fresh counterparts. In view of these additional costs, it is inevitable that changes would come to classic barrel aging in the form of new technologies.

Among these new tools that simulate the effects of barrel aging—without requiring the extended time and high costs of purchasing new barrels—are the mechanical introduction of oxygen (called micro-oxygenation), the addition of commercially available enological tannins, the addition of oak chips directly into the wine, and warming or chilling the cellar to speed or slow reactions.

Some less expensive but very good wines are made using these modern approaches to aging. On the other hand, it is doubtful that a wine made in this way has ever been scored 100 points by wine guru Robert Parker.

Like this handsome barrel-aging cellar at Penfolds in Australia, most modern cellars are controlled at 55 to 60°F (12.8 to 15.6°C) with 70 to 80 percent humidity to keep the resting wines in good condition.

Whichever methods are used, all wines eventually meet their date with the bottling line. Some will be in their "prime" and ready for the retail shelf after a short period of recovery from "bottle shock," while others will continue to age and develop in the bottle for many more years—either in the winery's warehouse or in the personal cellar of the collector or wine aficionado.

THE PRODUCTION OF AN OAK BARREL FOR WINEMAKING

Great barrels from little acorns grow.

Carefully tended oak forests produce straight and flawless trunks for use in barrel making.

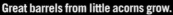

The trunks are marked for furniture-quality quarter-sawn stave material. Staves for top-quality and very expensive barrels are aged in the open air for eighteen to thirty-six months to encourage unique enzymatic action in the wood.

Once the staves are cut they are assembled in a tubelike shape and heated by a fire in the middle to soften and toast them.

As the staves warm they become soft, and modeling hoops are driven over them to create the classic barrel shape.

INTERVIEW WITH:
PETER GAGO
PENFOLDS, ADELAIDE, AUSTRALIA

MY EARLY IMPRESSIONS OF THE WIDE WORLD OF WINE CAME FROM MY FRANCOPHILE FATHER, WHO STEPPED WAY OUT TO EXPERIMENT WITH GERMAN WINES, THOUGHT ITALIAN WINES WERE TOO COMPLICATED, AND NEVER PUT A SPANISH WINE ON THE TABLE. IT WAS HARD TO FIND AUSTRALIAN WINES BACK THEN, SO MY FIRST EXPERIENCE WITH AUSTRALIA WAS A CONTRABAND RED A FRIEND BROUGHT BACK FROM A BUSINESS TRIP. HERMITAGE GRANGE, IT WAS CALLED, FROM PENFOLDS WINES PTY. LTD.

At the time, I had tasted my way across North America and through all of Europe's major appellations, from Lebanon to the soggy vineyards of southern England, but I had never tasted anything like this before. Big, dark fruit, brooding, incredibly concentrated, dry, smooth as a baby's backside with fine, grainy tannins. I thought I was drinking unsweetened Port. It was almost fifteen more years before I got a chance to taste a Grange again, and I probably needed the time to truly appreciate this incredible Australian wine.

Made in a style created by Max Schubert in the 1950s, Grange is listed by the National Trust of Australia as a Heritage Icon; it was lauded by revered wine scribe, Hugh Johnson, as the only "First Growth" of the Southern Hemisphere. Its creation is now entrusted to chief winemaker Peter Gago. I spoke to Peter twice during his harvest season and there was that unmistakable lack-of-sleep quality to his voice, yet I was amazed at his patience and ability to focus on the subject of aging wine when he was surrounded by a winery's equivalent to a thousand screaming babies.

Penfolds St. Henri, shown here in a 1956 bottling, is known to age gracefully for many years and is featured prominently in the sixth edition of the winery's profound Rewards of Patience publication.

The highly respected Grange Hermitage was created by Penfolds' then chief winemaker Max Schubert in 1955, and has served since as a model for this powerful style of Australian Shiraz.

PETER, I KNOW YOU MAKE MANY DIFFERENT WINES, BUT I THINK PEOPLE IDENTIFY PENFOLDS MOST WITH THE INCREDIBLE GRANGE. IS THAT GOOD OR BAD? TELL ME ABOUT THE GRANGE.

In Australia, for a long time, Grange was its own thing. It was so secular, different, individualistic in style. It was created almost sixty years ago and was quite unique in its day. We've never been arrogant enough to say this is Australia's best wine, but what we can say with qualification is that it's always been up there somewhere at the top end of the totem pole.

However, in the last few decades, there have been many other Australian winemakers who have adopted similar techniques and who have attempted to create similar styles. And of course, there are a few journalists and competitors who would like to see it fall from grace. That's the Australian psyche. I think in America you tend to reward success holistically, more generously. In Australia, we love the story of the underdog.

WHAT'S IT LIKE FOR YOU TO BE THE CUSTODIAN OF THIS NATIONAL TREASURE?

Actually, my job is relatively easy. The style is long since established. It's most dramatic evolution has already taken place. Now, refinement is the name of the game, trying to optimize what Mother Nature offers us in a given vintage.

When I became chief winemaker, a lot of journalists asked, what are you going to do? How are you going to change Grange? How are you going to make it better? And they were a little bit disappointed when I said I'm going to deliberately change absolutely nothing. With other wines I have more license to input, but the ego imprint is something that's quite scary when you're looking at revered generational wines and styles. Maybe you make slight adjustments, but you don't bounce off the walls in terms of stylistic change.

WERE YOU OKAY WITH THAT?

Yes, of course. Besides my position as winemaker at Penfolds, I'm also a wine lover and collector. I've now been drinking Grange for almost four decades, so I have a deep understanding and respect for this wine and its style.

But there's another layer of engagement in my role in that I am the leader of a very highly tuned and carefully mentored Penfolds winemaking team that makes many other wines. Grange may be the star, but there are other key players on the team.

SO TELL ME ABOUT THE OTHER PENFOLDS WINES. MY INTEREST IS IN BARREL AGING, SO WHAT PERCENTAGE OF PENFOLDS WINES ARE BARREL AGED?

I can't give you an exact number, because it depends on the various blend volumes we produce, which vary annually. But in reds, everything from our Koonunga Hill level up is barrel aged, literally everything. In the Barossa Valley we have a barrel facility that covers almost 5 acres (2 ha). In our whites, obviously Rieslings are not barrel aged, but all of our Chardonnays are.

WHAT DO YOU FEEL ARE THE BENEFITS OF BARREL AGING WINES?

There are two main functions of barrel aging. First is a gentle oxidative maturation over time (with varying times for different styles), and the ingress of oxygen, including polymerization and esterification. Second, there are other chemical reactions in the wine, due to, among other things, the impartation of oak-derived tannins.

DO YOU DIFFERENTIATE BETWEEN NEW AND OLDER OAK?

It depends on the style of the wine and the size of the barrel (surface area to volume ratio). Sometimes newer oak is incorporated because some winemakers prefer a modicum of cedarlike oak flavor in their wines. What we seek is the structural impact of new oak compared to older oak in certain wine styles.

HOW DOES THAT WORK?

As a generalization, new French oak tends to structurally tighten up the wine, adding another dimension. Some of this is due to the pickup of oak-derived tannin. On top of that, with whites in particular, there is contact with the gross lees (sediments). There's a great deal that happens in the barrel when you think about it—what's in the lees, CO_2 exchange, the different tannins, polysaccharides, and dynamics we don't know that much about—particularly when it comes to the exact nature such chemical and physical effects have on the maturing wine.

HOW ABOUT THE SIZE OF THE WOODEN CONTAINER? DOES THAT HAVE AN EFFECT?

Yes, of course. We might use a *barrique* (225 liters, or 60 gallons), a hogshead (300 liters, or 80 gallons), a puncheon (450 to 500 liters, or 120 to 132 gallons), or a large vat for aging different wines. That's all part of the decision-making process, and each year's growing conditions might cause different decisions. There is no formula, whether it's size of barrels or how long we keep it in barrel ... it's decision making all the way through, with stylistic templates offering direction.

YOU MENTIONED TIME IN BARRELS? WHAT DO YOU DO?

Grange might be in oak for as short as eighteen months or as long as twenty-plus months. So there can be a big spread! But we do have some rough rules for when we rack. Generally, when a wine has been in barrel on the gross lees for about six weeks, we start thinking about racking. So we taste, and maybe it's not ready yet and needs a bit more time. But there are certain alerts, certain cues that tell you to get the wine off the lees. That make you think about whether it's finished malolactic, so maybe it's time for its first racking. And then a little bit later on it's had two rackings. Now you're thinking, should we give it a third racking before bottling or has it had enough? Is it a lighter year? Is it a bigger year? Does it need to sort of settle down a bit more? It's all about style!

You know we make many different Shiraz styles. It would be a bit boring if they all looked the same, if they were all made similarly. It could be that one lot is from the Barossa Valley and one is from Coonawarra, but then we go further and we use American oak for one and French oak for another, one vat matured, one new-oak matured, one old-oak matured, one barrel fermented. You know all of those things are thrown into the mix, so there is not just one style I can talk about.

EXCEPT FOR MAYBE GRANGE?

Yes, that one is easy because by definition, Grange is always 100 percent new oak, *Quercus alba*, American oak! And for the person who likes French oak, we have an RWT Shiraz (Red Winemaking Trials) from the Barossa Valley that is a more contemporary style matured completely in French oak. This one has a little bit more emphasis on fruit and is a lovely contrast. And we have a third style, the St. Henri,

The beautiful Penfolds Winery reception center, surrounded by handsome old vines, showcases historic Australian architecture. Penfolds' famous slogan "1844 to evermore" refers to its founding by Dr. Christopher Rawson Penfold and his wife Mary—who farmed the original vineyards—in 1844.

that is matured in very large, oak vats, also very old, a minimum of fifty years, so in other words, the oak is no longer contributing. This is a style unencumbered by oak, unencumbered by oak flavor, unencumbered by oak-derived tannins—it is an old-fashioned style with a beautiful texture that just rolls off the tongue. It is made very differently than both the Grange and the RWT. And over the years, over the decades, a good vintage of St. Henri will age as well as a good vintage of Grange, so they are equally good, just different. And there's a fourth style of Shiraz ... but I think you get the point.

YES, I SEE WHAT YOU MEAN ABOUT USING DIFFERENT TYPES OF OAK AND DIFFERENT METHODS TO CREATE DIFFERENT STYLES OF WINES.

Yes, and we're only talking about Shiraz! We also do Bin 707, 100 percent Cabernet, and our Rhône blends of Grenache, Mourvèdre, and Shiraz ...

AND THEY'RE ALL BARREL AGED?

Yes, but they are all matured differently.

TAKING A DIFFERENT TACK, HOW DO YOU SORT IT ALL OUT—DECIDE WHICH GRAPES GO INTO WHICH LOTS, WHICH WILL BE BARREL FERMENTED, WHICH WILL MATURE IN LARGE VATS VS. SMALL BARRIQUES, WHICH IN NEW OAK, WHICH IN OLD OAK?

Well, we start by grading the fruit in the vineyard, A grade, B grade, C grade, and so on. Because you would never waste, for example, a new oak barrel on D-grade fruit, because you would just be wasting money. And that sorting is done primarily in the vineyards. It's followed by a tasting after harvest that we call a "classification" tasting. We start the classification at the top, with Grange, and then it's a cascading

Penfolds Wines Pty. Ltd. is large and versatile enough to barrel age in wood containers from large to small, depending on the winemaker's direction.

Some of Penfolds' richest and most distinguished red wines are born from old vine Shiraz that is grown in red clay soils.

effect downward (with some exceptions such as single-vineyard and single-region wines). We taste and determine which goes into new oak, old oak, American oak, and so on.

AND THEN HOW DO YOU DETERMINE WHAT GOES INTO GRANGE?

I make that decision after fermentation. A wine either has it or it doesn't. There is no fixing or changing it to be more like what it needs to be on paper!

OKAY, I GET THE PICTURE, BUT LET'S GO OUT IN LEFT FIELD… WHAT ARE YOUR FEELINGS ABOUT WOOD CHIPS AND ENOLOGICAL TANNIN ADDITION?

Personally, I don't feel these new "products" achieve what time-honored methods have proven to work in bottle, with aging. But if good-quality grapes are used, perhaps adding oak, tannins and bubbling oxygen through a wine (micro-oxygenation) can be looked at as another way of striving for similar effects as barrel aging.

The way I look at it is that winemaking is an ancient craft, and we don't really make wine much differently now than we made it twenty years ago or fifty years ago. Because it works. So if it's not broken…. Now inner-stave technology, wood chip technology, cheaper ways of doing this and/or not using oak at all—all of these have been trialed. But let's face it, what French First Growth doesn't use oak barrels? And what Napa Valley top-grade producer does not use the best oak they can access?

So it's not just fashion. There is something beyond just the flavor of the oak. It's about the dynamic, a living dynamic, a living interface and interaction among oak, oak-derived tannins, wine, oxygen ingress, the variable of time, all coming together to optimize what oak barrels offer.

YOU'VE GIVEN US A VERY CLEAR PICTURE OF WHAT BARREL AGING DOES FOR THE WINES. BUT WHAT DOES IT DO TO YOU?

For me, it's quite an evocative, alluring, "sirens beckoning you onto the rocks" sort of thing. There's nothing quite like getting to know a barrel of wine from its coarse beginnings, immediately after fermentation, and watching that wine evolve in barrel as you taste it and follow it all the way up through the day it's bottled and encased into a 750 ml glass container.

AND THEN WHAT? IS THERE LIFE AFTER BOTTLING?

Oh, yes. The journey of a wine is a wondrous one to follow, and it continues with bottle aging. A great wine is not something that is created suddenly one day. It is enjoyable to open a bottle of wine when it is five years old, when it is ten, twenty, or thirty years old. All the time it is evolving new flavors and texturally transforming, always revealing something different. I truly enjoy tasting older wines, but what I really enjoy is the evolution.

With its wooden bung tightly secured to prevent oxidation, this barrel of Penfolds Bin 707 Cabernet Sauvignon begins its long period of development in the cool cellar.

Spring is beautiful in this Penfolds vineyard, promising exciting wines to come. Penfolds has vineyards in Adelaide, Barossa Valley, McLaren Vale, Clare Valley, Coonawarra, and other sites in South Australia.

Workers in the Penfolds cellar "pump over" new red wines during their primary fermentation in old, open-topped concrete tanks.

FINALLY, IT'S GRADUATION DAY. OUR PROGENY IS GROWN UP AND ABOUT TO LEAVE THE CELLAR. THE ROUGH EDGES ARE NOW SMOOTH AND HAVE ATTAINED AN OBVIOUS DEGREE OF REFINEMENT.

CHAPTER 11:
THE FINAL FRONTIER: BOTTLING

At the Montes Winery in Chile, after wines are bottled and the decorative capsules applied, they are packed in shipping cases and aged for a minimum of six additional months in bottle.

The raw fruit and funky smells have given way to a new entity with depth and character. It's time to move on to the bottle, out of the cellar, into the warehouse, and, eventually, onto the retail shelf for the consumer who will enjoy it today or the collector who will store it for a later date.

WHEN TO BOTTLE?

When is that perfect moment to bottle a wine? What pulls the trigger? For the most part, wines are ready for bottling when the winemaker says they are ready—relying on years of academic studies, industry-wide accepted procedures, centuries of historic data, or just a sixth sense screaming "NOW!" But many factors play into and influence bottling decisions, as they do throughout every aspect of the winemaking journey.

STABILITY

When wine goes into the bottle it needs to be clear and free of active yeast or bacteria. Cloudy wines are unattractive, bacterial infections (such as vinegar) cause off smells and flavors, and who hasn't heard about bottles that have exploded or corks that push out when active yeast cells mate with residual sugar in the bottle? All bottled wines will eventually throw down some type of sediment, but it is the winemaker's goal to have achieved a degree of stability for at least a few years.

If previous cellar procedures and the modest use of sulfur dioxide (a.k.a. sulfites) have not already accomplished this by the time the wine is headed to the bottling line, various types of filtration and other options are available. But they are used with caution because of the fear of sacrificing or losing "good stuff" in the wine along with the bad.

STYLE

When any given wine style or variety of grape has achieved the desired balance of smells, tastes, and textures, there is nothing further to be gained by keeping it in barrels or tanks. Now it will benefit most by being bottled and allowed to continue aging in the bottle.

If a wine needs to be filtered it is typically done immediately before bottling. This plate and frame filter (designed to remove large sediments) is being used in conjunction with a membrane cartridge filter.

But every style has its own timetable! Some of the lightest, fruity red wines, such as Beaujolais Nouveaux, are bottled in fall only a few weeks after harvest. Many exciting young Rieslings from the Mosel and Rhine regions of Germany fairly scream to be bottled just months after fermentation to capture their irresistible terroir and lively fresh fruit. In contrast are the many months, even years of gestating a complex Nebbiolo or opulent Tempranillo, patiently waiting for the change of life as it slowly develops from harsh to smooth, from simplicity to multitiered layers of complexity.

TRADITION

Some older wine regions have long-standing traditions and established legal definitions that dictate how long certain wines will be aged before bottling. In Rioja, Spain, for instance, a wine labeled "Crianza" means it has been barrel aged a minimum of a year before bottling. "Reserva" means at least three years of barrel and bottle aging before release, with a minimum of one year in barrel. In Italy, wines grown in Montalcino can only be called "Brunello di Montalcino" if they have been barrel aged at least two years and bottle aged another two.

PRAGMATISM AND ECONOMIC PRESSURE

But there are other less esoteric reasons for bottling. When I lived in Burgundy, some of my neighbors in the village of Montrachet told me the reason they bottle their wines in late summer is to empty barrels so they will be available for the arrival of the new vintage in fall. It was simply practical and economically advantageous to do this. Likewise, many producers around world bottle wines on a schedule that allows them to clear out the cellar to make way for the new vintage—or to stock the shelves or warehouse if supplies are running low.

This membrane cartridge filter is valued for its absolute pore size and ability to retain and remove unwanted yeast or bacteria from wine immediately before it goes into the bottle.

The need for income or to fill lines of distribution does not trump whether or not a wine is ready to be bottled, but it would be misleading not to acknowledge this type of pressure from the sales and marketing side or the accounting department. It is a delicate dance, with many repercussions for all concerned. To give just one example, bottling prematurely might mean locking in tannins so massive that the wine remains harsh, which, in turn, affects its marketability.

WHAT IS INVOLVED IN THE BOTTLING PROCESS?

The essence of bottling is getting wine from a bulk vessel or barrel into a smaller, sealed container—stable and in condition to be consumed now or to continue maturing gracefully in the bottle. "When" has already been addressed, but a few other questions will explain the process.

WHAT?

In most wineries, "bottling" is actually "packaging"—and involves not only putting the wine into bottle (or other receptacles, such as the new "bag in the box" plastic containers) but also applying the closure (cork, stopper, or screw cap), the capsule (decorative metal or plastic cover), and the label(s). It may be (and usually is) done with a mechanized bottling line, but in some cases this is done by hand.

WHERE?

Most wineries bottle on their own premise, but for those without bottling facilities, mobile bottling lines travel to the winery location in many areas. Other wines may leave the winery premise entirely and travel to a designated facility that has equipment for specialty packages, such as small 175 ml splits or bag-in-the-box technology.

Even when wines are bottled on the winery premise, circumstances range from large pressurized sterile bottling rooms to a tiny corner of the cellar or a dilapidated barn. Although the first scenario seems much more desirable, time, innovation, and determination have proven that successful bottling can be achieved in a wide variety of places and spaces.

HOW?

First, the lot or cuvée is assembled and assessed, and any final corrections are made. Then it is propelled via pumps and hoses or permanent lines into the bottling equipment, beginning with the filler. The hoses and tubing used to get the wine to the filler are usually cleaned and sterilized by hot water or steam. Assuming the bottles arrive from the factory sterilized (by the high temperature of manufacture), the trick is to ensure that contamination doesn't occur any time before the filled bottle is sealed. Thus, just before filling, cloudy wines or wines with sugar or nutrients enough to referment are usually filtered through a micron cartridge with pore size tight enough to retain sediments, yeast, or bacteria.

The next step is inserting the cork or applying a closing device. Then, unless the sealed bottles are destined to be laid down for further bottle aging, the wines receive their decorative capsule and labels.

THE GREAT DEBATES: WHAT KIND OF PACKAGE IS BEST?

There is an ongoing debate in the wine industry that pits tradition against convenience. On one side are those who say you lose the "romance" of wine without a glass bottle and cork; on the other side are those favoring cheaper packaging that doesn't require a corkscrew!

GLASS BOTTLES VERSUS PLASTIC CONTAINERS
Many hundreds of years ago wines were sealed in amphora (ceramic pots) or toted around in goatskins. In the seventeenth century, glass bottle manufacturing became commercial and wine was found to mature successfully in various shapes and sizes. Today wine is also bottled into plastic pouches or bottles and large metal-lined "bag-in-a-box" containers (or "casks" in Australia).

Which is preferable depends a great deal on the individual consumer and the intended use. What has been established is that glass is a standard we know, understand, and accept because it can be cleaned, adds no flavor, and allows no passage of oxygen, except at the closure. Wines with keeping properties can age for decades in glass.

Plastic containers, even those that are metal lined, eventually allow oxygen to penetrate and come into contact with the wine. Thus, they are best as short-term storage devices, somewhere in the range of five to ten months. On the other hand, they are cheap, convenient, and leave a small carbon footprint!

On the bottling line at Chaddsford Winery, the bottles have been rinsed and now the wine is being forced into the bottle under very low pressure seconds before the bottle is corked.

A cellar worker prepares a plate and frame filter prior to bottling; the wine will be gently pumped through cellulose pads for clarification.

CORKS VERSUS SCREW CAPS

The reason for a closure is to keep wine from leaking and to minimize oxygen absorption during bottle aging of the wine. The traditional wood cork is a plug from the bark of an oak tree that allows minimum oxygen ingress. Ideally, it won't leak unless stored upright for twelve to eighteen months, causing the cork to dry out, shrink, and lose its seal. Depending on the quality of corks used, they are known to be serviceable between fifteen and twenty-five years.

For many wine drinkers, a traditional wood cork is part of the history and "romance" of drinking wine. In addition, today's consumer appreciates the environmentally beneficial and sustainable aspects of a natural product such as cork. On the other hand, two disadvantages of using a traditional cork are (1) it can be flawed or damaged in bottling, allowing air to eventually contact the wine, and (2) occasionally, a mold within the cork will come into contact with the wine and destroy its character (this is referred to as the wine being "corked").

Among the many other types of stoppers used today are agglomerate corks made of molded bits of natural cork and several types of synthetic corks made of extruded plastics or silicone. Such synthetic stoppers are still being perfected; although they do not leak wine, they are known to leak oxygen after three to six years—making them well suited for wines meant to be drunk young. The big advantage of such stoppers is that they are less expensive than traditional high-quality cork, do not taint the wine, and are less prone to breakage.

Another big player in the modern closure game is the screw cap, with more than fifty years of technology and experience behind it. Once the dominion of only the lowest quality wines, screw caps (as well as attractive and elegant glass closures) are today being used successfully by many top-quality, uber-expensive wines. Notwithstanding the painful break in tradition and the irrepressible urge to use a corkscrew, many oenophiles now believe that screw caps and glass stoppers are definite contenders as ideal long-term storage closures.

I'LL HAVE A METHUSELAH, PLEASE ...

How big are wine bottles?
About as big as you want!

A Standard Wine Bottle holds
0.75 liter of wine = One bottle

A Magnum Wine Bottle holds 1.5 liters of wine = Two bottles

A Jeroboam Wine Bottle holds 3 liters of wine = Four bottles

A Rehoboam Wine Bottle holds 4.5 liters of wine = Six bottles

A Methuselah Wine Bottle holds 6 liters of wine = Eight bottles

A Salmanazar Wine Bottle holds 9 liters of wine = Twelve bottles

A Balthazar Wine Bottle holds 12 liters of wine = Sixteen bottles

A Nebuchadnezzar Wine Bottle holds 15 liters of wine = Twenty bottles

CORK PRODUCTION

Once it reaches its 25th year, the thick loose bark of *Quercus subur*, a species of oak tree, is cut and harvested for wine corks. Most of the world's cork comes from Portugal, Spain, Algeria, and Morocco.

When the trees are stripped of the cork bark, it is stacked on pallets and brought to the factory for cleaning and sorting.

Supreme Corq has been a leading manufacturer of synthetic wine bottle closures that avoid cork taint and seal off oxygen for three to six years of bottle aging; such "corks" also provide a modern design edge with their bright colors and graphics.

A punt refers to the concave bottom of wine bottles. It is a historical remnant from the era when bottles were free blown using a blowpipe; theories about its origin and use range from strength and stability to consolidation of sediments in a ring at the bottom of the bottle. A punt serves no practical purpose today, but many consumers see its presence as an indication of quality.

After the cork bark has been cleaned, it is cut into strips from which the actual pieces of cork will be punched out.

Now that the cork bark has been cut into strips, corks for use in the wine industry are punched out with a razor-sharp cylinder.

The perfect cork compresses without cracking, expands to seal within minutes of being inserted into the neck of the bottle, and has no fungus or mildew that would cause "cork taint" if in contact with wine.

Once wines are bottled, it's off to the warehouse for short-term recovery from the "jolting" bottling experience (often called "bottle shock"), or, in some cases, longer term storage for a period of "bottle aging."

Although the Montes Winery now has vineyards and winemaking operations in Argentina and California, its first plantings were in the dramatic wine regions of Chile, including Apalta and Marchigue in the Colchagua Valley.

INTERVIEW WITH:
AURELIO MONTES
MONTES WINERY, SANTIAGO, CHILE

I WAS FIRST OFFERED THE BRILLIANT WINES OF AURELIO MONTES OF CHILE WHILE ON LAYOVER IN PUERTO RICO DURING A WINTER GETAWAY. SINCE THEN, I ASSOCIATE FLEEING THE COLD WITH ENJOYING MONTES WINERY'S CONTINUALLY EXPANDING AREAS OF DISTRIBUTION, FROM MEXICO TO THE DOMINICAN REPUBLIC TO PANAMA AND COSTA RICA. NOW IT'S LIKE MEETING AN OLD FRIEND AT EVERY PORT AS AVAILABILITY OF THE DYNAMIC MONTES WINES HAS SPREAD TO THE U.K., MAINLAND EUROPE, ACROSS THE UNITED STATES, AND AS FAR AS KAZAKHSTAN!

It isn't surprising that a grape-friendly region such as Chile makes such good wines, only that it took so long to establish once and for all time its high-quality potential in the international wine scene. Chile was first planted with wine grapes in the mid-sixteenth century by the Spanish conquistadors and has continuously provided for expanding consumption of its own modest wines. The wine industry declined during the political unrest of the 1970s. Then, as the likes of Aurelio Montes invested in large plantings and modern wineries, Chile came back in the 1980s with a delicious tide of table wines that were quickly discovered.

As chief winemaker and president of Montes Winery, Aurelio Montes is personally responsible for ensuring the quality of all the Montes wines from Chile, Argentina, and most recently, California. His stellar winemaking career has spanned three decades, and today he stands at the forefront of the Chilean wine industry, defining his country's new image of quality.

Perched high in the Colchagua appellation of Chile, the state-of-the-art Montes Apalta Winery produces Cabernet Sauvignon, Merlot, Carmenere, Chardonnay, and Sauvignon Blanc.

AURELIO, TELL ME ABOUT YOUR WINEMAKING BACKGROUND AND THE STORY OF MONTES WINERY.

I started in the Catholic University in Santiago. In Chile, you have to be an agronomist, an agricultural engineer, before you can apply for winemaking as a specialty. I graduated in 1972 as an agronomist with a specialty in vineyards and winemaking, and then worked for five years at a very big winery and then another twelve years as chief winemaker for another very well-known Chilean winery.

AND HOW DID MONTES COME TO BE?

After those seventeen years, I joined with three partners and we decided to establish our own business, aiming primarily at high-quality wines. I felt it was perfectly possible to produce them in Chile, but no one was doing that at the time. We started our adventure in 1988, doing both high-end reds and whites, and it was quite a success. Now, we are the fourth largest winery in Chile—in terms of exports—with a very high reputation in terms of quality in all of our lines of wines.

I'M SURE IT WASN'T AS EASY AS YOU MAKE IT SOUND! HOW DID YOU ACHIEVE THIS SUCCESS SO QUICKLY?

We grew! In 2002 we thought that we could spread our wings a bit farther than just Chile, so we crossed the Andes Mountains to Argentina and established our winery in Mendoza, Kaiken—named for the wild goose that flies freely from Chile to Argentina. It's a Patagonian bird that is very pretty. I like the symbolism, because we also "fly" between those two countries, for winemaking purposes.

Then in 2006, we felt that we had some extra energy to burn, so we moved to Napa Valley and started an operation there. Our first wine was a Cabernet Sauvignon from Napa, and then, for our second vintage, we added a Syrah from the Central Coast, near Paso Robles.

Over the course of his thirty-year career, Aurelio Montes, chief wine-maker and president of Montes Winery in Chile, has received a vast number of international awards for his exemplary work. He also consults, teaches, and lectures around the world on behalf of Montes and Chilean wines.

The "evergreen" partners at Montes Winery in Chile have committed to using new eco-friendly lightweight bottles as a measure to help preserve the surrounding ecosystem and environment. Montes also utilizes sustainable agriculture in their vineyards.

I UNDERSTAND THAT YOU NOW EXPORT MONTES WINES TO MORE THAN A HUNDRED COUNTRIES, WHICH MEANS YOU HAVE A VERY BUSY BOTTLING PROGRAM. HOW DO YOU MAKE SURE THAT EVERY BOTTLE IS PERFECT, THAT IT'S WHAT YOU WERE SHOOTING FOR?

First of all, as we approach bottling, we have our blends all totally stable in terms of tartrates and microbiology. The winemaking team has checked everything thoroughly. Then at the moment when we decide to bottle, we try to do the least shaking of the wine, perform the fewest operations, so as not to stress the wine.

We bottle straight from the tank. No intermediate holding tank, no filters. In order to avoid all that "stress," we just move the wine with stainless steel pipelines, straight to the bottling line. There we do a membrane (micron) filtration only (no pads), to keep the wine as untouched as possible. This helps keep the quality, the power, and the integrity of the wine inside the bottle.

WHAT TYPE OF TESTS DO YOU DO BEFORE BOTTLING?

We test for clarity and we do microbiology [tests], to see if there is any sort of contamination. But we are a very neat winery: We clean our tanks and plants thoroughly, so we have very low contamination. If we felt there was a need, we would do a diatomaceous earth (rough) filtration. Usually we can rely on the membrane filter, which will get rid of any yeast or bacteria. And then it's on to the bottle!

TELL ME, AS A WINEMAKER, HOW YOU MAKE THE DECISION TO BOTTLE THE WINE AT A PARTICULAR TIME? WHAT ARE THE FACTORS THAT YOU ARE BALANCING AND WEIGHING?

We normally keep a portion of our wines in barrels, and a certain proportion in stainless steel. The final blend captures a little bit of the fruit, coming from the stainless steel, with complexity and finesse coming from the barrels. There is no exact time frame when the total aging process is finished, but I try to keep the reds in bulk for two full winters. That allows for the natural precipitation of tartrates so the wine is stable without the need to do cold stabilization—although we cold stabilize the whites.

When all that is done, then we want to get wines into the bottle as fast as possible. I am a big believer in bottle age.

WOULD YOU DISCUSS BOTTLE AGING FURTHER?

In my opinion, the wine continues to develop after bottling and the amount of complexity it gains in the bottle is enormous. You can already see this evolution when you open the bottle after the first month. After a year of bottle aging, the wine starts to gain complexity. Depending on the wine, this process can be positive for at least ten years.

WHAT CAUSES THIS CONTINUED DEVELOPMENT IN THE BOTTLE?

During barrel aging we obtain oxidation of the wine when tiny bits of oxygen permeate through the barrel staves. But during bottle aging, the wine suffers the opposite, which is the reduction of the wine. So in the first case, oxygen is being added, and in the second case, it is being reduced. This process enhances the bouquet and develops secondary flavors, which add to the complexity.

SO HOW LONG DO YOU KEEP THE WINES IN BOTTLE BEFORE RELEASING THEM?

Normally, we try to achieve not less than six months in the bottle before the wine is released.

DOES PRESSURE FROM THE MARKETPLACE EVER DETERMINE WHEN YOU BOTTLE, OR WHEN YOU RELEASE THE WINES?

Yes, certainly—we are a part of the world, and the market has certain behaviors, which can be demanding. But we base our decision on quality first. The wine is bottled when we feel it is ready, and released after aging for six months in the bottle. If for some reason we are out of a wine and the next vintage is not yet available to meet market demand, we ask our customers to be patient and wait until the wine has developed sufficiently according to our standards.

IN YOUR LONG HISTORY OF MAKING WINE, HAVE YOU EVER MADE A SIGNIFICANT ERROR IN BOTTLING A PARTICULAR WINE?

Oh, yes. Of course. I can recall many years ago while I was a winemaker at another winery, we had a problem with the cleaning solution that had been used to wash the bottling system. Some of the material we were using that day went into the line and it was a big disaster because we had about five thousand or six thousand bottles that were totally contaminated with this solution. This iodine-like characteristic was quite evident in the wine, so we had to reopen all those bottles. It was a big lesson—it happened once, but never again!

THAT'S THE KIND OF THING THAT MAKES YOU FEEL BAD AFTER A BOTTLING. BUT WHAT'S THE GOOD SIDE? WHAT'S SATISFYING ABOUT BOTTLING WINES?

It's very satisfying to reach the end, to have gone through the complete winemaking process. To work with the wine in barrels and tanks and spend two years with it. To know the wine is well made, neat, clean, and it doesn't have any sort of contamination. To know you have achieved a certain quality. It is quite satisfying to finally put that wine in a bottle with your name on it because you know perfectly well its behavior will be astonishing in the future.

Most wines benefit from decanting to allow oxygen contact (to "open up" the wine) and separate any sediments in the bottle.

FROM PLANTING A VINEYARD THROUGH REAPING THE HARVEST, FROM BARREL AGING THROUGH THE BOTTLING PROCESS—WE HAVE TAKEN A LONG WINEMAKING JOURNEY TOGETHER. WE HAVE EXPLORED THE ROLE OF THE WINEMAKER AND THE MANY DECISIONS THAT MUST BE MADE FROM THE FIRST VISION OF A COVETED WINE TO THE FINAL PRODUCT.

CHAPTER 12:
IN THE LABORATORY

In almost every part of the process, we have emphasized differences: different regions and climates, different grape varieties, different winemaking styles and traditions, different philosophies about fining and filtering, different types of aging. We have pointed out that winemaking is part science and part art, accounting for so many unique and wonderful wines being made around the world.

But there is one part of winemaking that is not vague, not open to interpretation—but rather exact and measurable. Quantitative rather than qualitative. This is the laboratory, the place that winemakers turn to for information, hard numbers, and a potentially different perspective before making important decisions. I think of lab data like an architect's measurements. You already have the vision. You can see it and feel it and taste it, but you need the facts to construct it properly.

Many wineries have their own in-house laboratory, run by trained enologists, while others send their samples to independent outside labs that specialize in winemaking. Some high-quality wineries that contract large quantities of different grapes from a broad range of soils and climates may even have multiple labs employing both technicians and research scientists. Just how much the lab is used varies tremendously between New World regions without long histories—which use the lab virtually every step of the way—and Old World wineries that have long records and traditions to use as guideposts.

WHAT HAPPENS IN THE LABORATORY?

The lab has an active role year-round. Its job is to provide information, monitor development, establish trends, and create a baseline for future reference. Although such analysis is often just a "touchstone" to confirm a decision already based on the palate, it is particularly significant when addressing anything new (such as an atypical vintage or a new variety) or when doing limited trials (rather than experimenting with an entire lot).

The key times for utilizing a lab are (1) during the final stages of ripening on the vine, (2) initial juice analysis at crush, (3) during fermentation, (4) as the wine evolves in the cellar, (5) when preparing for bottling, and (6) about seven days post-bottling.

Some lab testing is specific to one stage or another, but many of the elements being monitored are watched closely throughout the entire process of winemaking. It can be confounding, not only because these elements are interdependent, but also because at different stages in a wine's development they *create* significant features and at other times they *are* the significant features.

In the laboratory, wines are studied, sampled, and evaluated in neutral circumstances. Good information from the lab helps the winemaker make crucial decisions throughout the entire winemaking process.

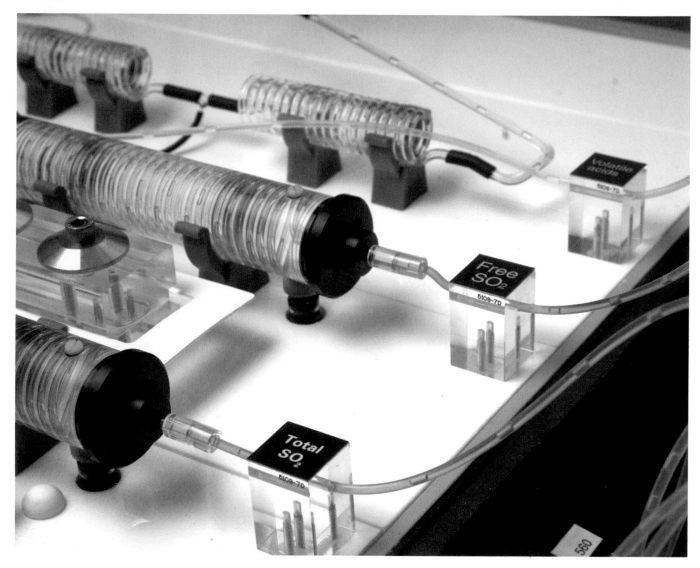

The following factors are monitored in the lab.

SUGAR

Sugar (measured as Brix, specific gravity, Baume, or Oechsle) is converted into alcohol and CO_2 during fermentation. It is monitored in the vineyard to help determine when picking should begin, and throughout the wine's life in the cellar because it is food for good and bad yeast and bacteria. In a finished wine, unfermented sugar will soften the perception of sharp acidity and harsh tannin.

ACIDITY

Acidity (measured as pH and as grams per liter of tartaric or sulfuric acid) preserves the wine, affects fermentations by yeast and bacteria, and contributes to balance in the finished wine.

ALCOHOL

Alcohol (most accurately measured by distillation) is produced when yeast consumes sugar in the fresh grape must. It eventually stops being produced when it's high enough to kill the yeast or it runs out of food. It is closely monitored during the fermentation period in case adjustments need to be made. Alcohol (at levels of 8.5 to 15 percent) inhibits some microorganisms, and also gives a sense of body or thickness to the wine while lifting smells and flavors.

Vinquiry, a sophisticated laboratory in Sonoma County, California, uses continuous flow analysis to test for sulfur dioxide (SO_2) and volatile acids. This procedure measures chemical reactions that occur in a continuous stream of wine divided by air bubbles.

NITROGEN

Nitrogen, in the range of 200 to 350 parts per million, is a key nutrient in grape juice. It does not directly contribute to a wine's flavor in that it is (ideally) fully consumed by a healthy fermentation so it is later unavailable to unwanted microorganisms.

SULFUR DIOXIDE (SO$_2$)

SO$_2$ (also known as sulfites) is added to wines to preserve color and inhibit unwanted yeast and bacteria early in a wine's life. Its effectiveness is dependent on the level of pH in the wine. Overuse of sulfites can actually damage a wine's color, give the wine a harsh mouthfeel, and—for some people—cause an allergic reaction. Thus, monitoring SO$_2$ can be crucial before bottling. A large decline in SO$_2$ after bottling might indicate microbiological activity.

CARBON DIOXIDE (CO$_2$)

CO$_2$ is a by-product of fermentation and helps preserve still wines. As it slowly comes out of suspension during the aging process, it helps sustain acidity and provides a blanket that separates the wine from oxygen. An increase of CO$_2$ post-bottling is a sign of unwanted microbiological activity. However, in sparkling wines, retention of CO$_2$ is necessary for the "bubbles."

YEAST AND BACTERIA

Yeast and bacteria are monitored by what they produce (e.g., alcohol) and/or by culturing a population (a cell or colony) in the lab both before and after bottling. Whether native or selected commercial strains are used, bacteria and yeast ferment to reduce acid, produce alcohol, and create smells, flavors, and textures. The important thing is knowing the good organisms from the bad ones, and when and how to address them.

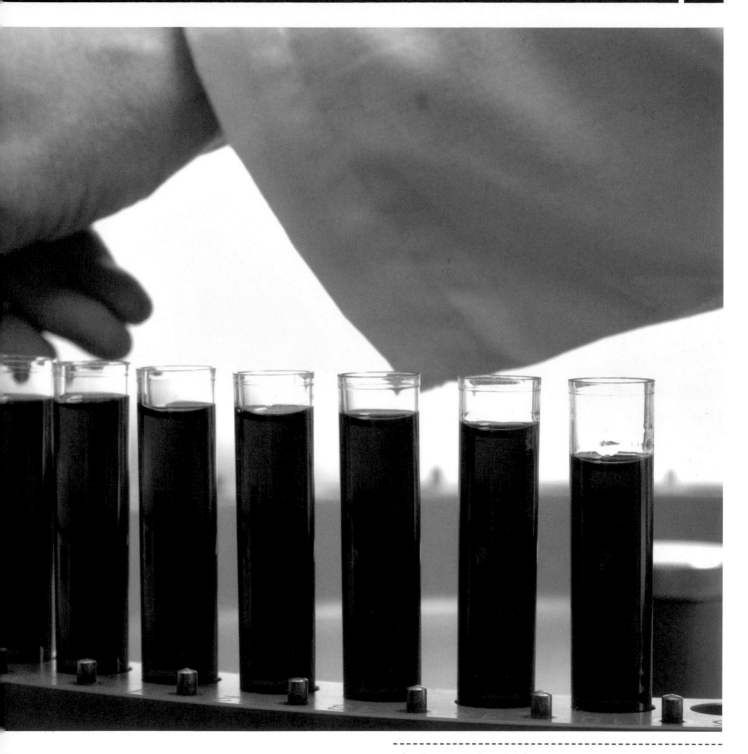

The Vinquiry Lab in California uses a process called NIR (Near InfraRed) for measuring alcohol. NIR measures the amount of light absorbed at specific frequencies to compute the percentage of alcohol in the wine sample.

VINEGAR (VOLATILE ACIDITY)
Vinegar is produced by bacteria. In a small quantity it is necessary to enrich a wine's smell and flavor. But because it is so sharp, a tiny excess amount of it can ruin a wine; thus, it is typically monitored and carefully controlled as cellars warm up in spring.

TARTRATES (POTASSIUM BITARTRATE)
Tartrates are salts that are unstable in alcoholic wines. Time and low temperature encourage precipitation of tartrates in the tank or barrel rather than later in the bottle. Although tartrates are harmless, most consumers consider them a flaw in the wine if they precipitate in the bottle.

PROTEIN
Affected by pH, alcohol, salts, and a host of things naturally found in wine, this occasional precipitate is light, flocculent, and ugly in the bottle. It is not surprising that winemakers routinely test for protein a few weeks before bottling.

THE END OF THE LINE
As long as there is wine, winemakers will be driven to understand the complex relationships and mysteries that surround it. The list above covers some of the basic elements of wine that are routinely monitored by the laboratory, but there are countless other tests that may also be run with the proper equipment: tests for color, tannins, haze, colloids … you name it.

These incubated micro trials require sophisticated lab equipment that the ordinary small winery does not have. Commercial laboratories are readily available in most wine-producing areas to perform such tests.

Even after thousands of years, winemakers are still finding new things about wine that drive them crazy, that keep them caught up in a restless codependency between gut feeling and the hard numbers of the laboratory.

One thing you will not find disputed, however, among the cast of characters who produce great wines around the world, is the passion shared by all. It's still amazing to me how each spring's joyous optimism morphs into creative high energy at harvest time, then becomes humble measurable knowledge a few years later … or perhaps a few hundred years later.

Natural crystals of potassium bitartrate—commonly called tar-trates—will precipitate in the bottle or form on corks if wines are not cold stable when bottled

One piece of testing equipment routinely used in winemaking is the hydrometer; it measures the Brix, or sugar level, of the grapes when they arrive on the processing deck and/or in the lab.

INTERVIEW WITH:
JOHANNES SELBACH
SELBACH-OSTER, MOSEL, GERMANY

MY INTEREST IN GERMAN WINES WAS PIQUED MANY YEARS AGO WHEN I WAS AN INEXPERIENCED WINEMAKER SEEKING TO BOTTLE A SWEET WINE THAT WOULD NOT REFERMENT IN THE BOTTLE. I HAD RECENTLY SAMPLED SOME SWEET WINES THAT BURNED MY NOSE WITH EXCESS SULFUR DIOXIDE, SO I WAS WORRIED ABOUT USING/MISUSING PRESERVATIVES. I HAD READ THAT SOME GERMAN WINEMAKERS WERE FILTERING TO REMOVE YEAST RATHER THAN KILLING THEM WITH CHEMICALS, SO I DECIDED TO GIVE IT A TRY.

I bought a steam genny, sterilized my hoses and six-spout gravity filler, prayed the barn rafters would hold, mounted a 500-gallon (1893 L) tank in the attic, pressurized it with CO_2, and forced what I then called "spring wine" through an 0.45 pharmaceutical-grade filter, and bingo—techno-nirvana. Nothing but pure fruit.

Johannes Selbach, whose family has been growing wine in the Mosel Valley of Germany since the sixteenth century, says he belongs in the conservative school that "does not fuss" much with the wines. In the vineyard, everything from pruning to harvesting is done by hand.

Germany has long been the source of superb winemaking equipment and exacting innovations in lab equipment. So when Terry Theis, perhaps the world's most respected importer of artisan German wines, referred me to Johannes Selbach of the Mosel Valley, I could almost taste the perfect, pure, minerally fruit of his Bernkasteler Riesling. I could see him in his white lab coat, bent over spiraling glass tubes, peering into his digital readouts, unlocking the scientific mysteries of his sterilized tanks of liquid refinement. … or not.

What I found instead was a brilliant, disciplined, Old World winemaker who relies first on four hundred years of experience in his family's vineyards. Although he is a trained and sophisticated winemaker in his own right, his take on the use of the laboratory spun me a complete 180. Johannes's philosophy of winemaking, he told me, is: "Hands-on in the vineyard; hands off in the cellar."

JOHANNES, I WAS KNOCKED OUT WHEN I HEARD THAT WEINGUT SELBACH-OSTER MAKES 12,500 CASES ANNUALLY AND 98 PERCENT OF IT IS RIESLING!

Our whole operation is about Riesling. It's a family business dating back to the year 1600 … and it's still about making true-to-type Riesling.

HOW DO YOU DEFINE "TRUE-TO-TYPE" RIESLING?

We consider Mosel Riesling to be defined by—here comes that ubiquitous French word—terroir.

Weingut Selbach-Oster looks the part of a traditional, centuries-old Mosel Valley winery. Like many wineries in the region, it grows and produces primarily Riesling wines.

For us, it is fruit and complexity in an elegant, not-so-alcoholic package. Riesling is the native grape that is indigenous to the central European river valleys; it is well adapted to the moderate climate and long growing seasons and rocky terrain. It produces a wine that shows unique characteristics that can best be described as a combination of minerality from the slate soil and delicate fruit.

Everything about Mosel is elegance and refinement. This is what we try to capture in our wines; it is very important for me personally—and has been important for my father and my grandfather through the generations. We believe in wines that make you smack your lips, that draw you back for more—not glitzy, bigger-is-better wines.

Selbach-Oster is an excellent vineyard site in the heart of the Mosel region, with old, ungrafted vines on steep, southern-facing slopes that are planted on heat-retaining, mineral-rich, rocky slate soils.

IN NEW WORLD WINERIES, WE'RE STILL EXPERIMENTING AND FIGURING OUT WHAT WE BELIEVE IN.

Here we have a track record of nearly two thousand years. Things happen differently here from places that have only a thirty-year or even fifty-year tradition. The vineyards we work with were planted 1,800 years, 1,900 years ago. And the knowledge about them and what they do well and what they do not so well has been passed down from generation to generation. We can make our winemaking decisions based on our senses, our intuition, the great stores of experience handed down rather than on using the laboratory to tell us what to do.

SINCE YOU MENTIONED THE SUBJECT OF LABORATORIES, DO YOU HAVE A LAB AT YOUR WINERY?

No, we don't have a lab. Of course, we do the basic analysis. We can test raw statistics: acidity, alcohol, sugars, SO_2, and we can keep an eye on volatile acidity. Everything else we give to a professional lab—they are specialists, so if we have a very special question or a problem, we will consult them.

But since we deal basically only with one grape, and only with white wines, there is not very much need of a big lab.

CAN YOU EXPLAIN THE CHEMICAL ANALYSIS THAT IS REQUIRED BY GERMAN LAW? I BELIEVE IT IS CALLED THE A.P. NUMBER (*AMTLICHE PRÜFUNGSNUMMER*) OR "OFFICIAL APPROVAL NUMBER."

Each German "quality" wine (QbA, meaning "quality," and QmP, meaning "highest quality") must be submitted to a professional lab and then to a tasting board, where they blind taste and smell, say it's okay, and assign it points. You have to reach a minimum points score in order to be released for sale. It's a combination of chemical analysis plus taste tests, and once you pass you can sell the wine.

The A.P. testing is for the finished wines, but of course there is testing the whole way through, beginning in the vineyard. We do know our grapes—and that is not just sweet talk (ha ha). But still when we pick, we visit our grapes almost daily to measure the sugar, look at the acidity. In the end, what really determines when we pick is how they taste.

"We can make our winemaking decisions based on our senses, our intuition, the great stores of experience handed down, rather than on using the laboratory to tell us what to do."

In the winery, during the production, we rely on what we know. We know the degrees of sweetness, we know the acidity. We prefer to ferment with indigenous yeast. We let things go. We listen, we taste, we check things, we make charts, but we don't really have any dramatic up and downs, so we stick with what we know. This is how we do it and how most people I know do it. End of story.

HOW ABOUT PUTTING THE WINES IN THE BOTTLE? DO YOU TEST FOR PROTEINS OR ANY OTHER THING THAT COULD PRECIPITATE IN THE BOTTLE? DO YOU WORRY ABOUT THAT?

Yes, before bottling I want to have a complete analysis. But that is part of the A.P. standard lab analysis—whether the wine is stable, whether the protein might fall out. We are routinely told by the lab the wine needs 2 kilos (4.4 pounds) of bentonite, or 3 kilos (6.6 pounds) of bentonite. But in fact, we never fine!

Once I was a guest at a very nice, high-reputed Riesling producer in the United States. We tasted the wine from the tank and the wine was wonderful. I was there with some colleagues and we said, "Oh, very nice wine, now you just need to bottle it." And he says, "No, no, no, we still need to fine it." We say, "What? You need to fine it? Why do you want to put in bentonite?" And he says, "Well, the lab says we need to put in bentonite; we always put in bentonite."

But that is a sin for us! We never touch the wine. If you want to do something, do it to the juice, but never touch the wine!

I THINK FINING IS ALWAYS A SOURCE OF DISAGREEMENT AMONG WINEMAKERS.

Yes, it is the way you are taught. If you were taught by a professor at a university, you would shake your head at some of the traditions in the Old World. But here, it is what my father told me, and what our old winemaker told me. They say don't worry about it if the lab says it's not stable, just go ahead and bottle it. And since they didn't go broke, I trusted them and I've done it that way for twenty years now.

AND YOU'VE NEVER HAD ANY PROBLEMS IN THE BOTTLE?

Oh, yes we have. But we take the risk and if any tartrates or sediments fall out, we put a back label on the bottle and say it's a natural product! It is okay to occasionally have a deposit. That is better than overtreating the wine.

DOES THAT MEAN YOU DON'T FILTER YOUR WINES EITHER?

We do filter, absolutely—we have to filter the sweet wines. We used to do no filtration, but then I had a problem with a wine that only had .02 percent residual sugar, bone-dry according to the lab. So we bottled it and it looked crystal clear and it was good for four months. Then comes the heat of the summer and that one or two yeast cells that were still in the bottle decided they would have to ferment that tiny bit of residual sugar. And the corks started popping and I definitely had a problem!

But we try to minimize it so that it is just one filtration when it goes into the bottle. There are people who put it three, four times through the filter and every time they lose flavor. That's why we don't use all the technology, which is very common in large wineries. If I made five million gallons, yes, but we're small potatoes. If I filter too much I would lose the delicacy, the fruit. And that is what Riesling is all about.

YOUR WINES SPEAK FOR THEMSELVES AND SHOW BEAUTIFULLY. AND YOU ARE ABSOLUTELY CONSISTENT— FROM THE DESCRIPTION OF HOW YOU DO IT TO THE WAY YOU FEEL ABOUT YOUR WINES.

Maybe I am a little bit of a wine freak. It has fascinated me from my teenage years and my family has ignited the fire in me. And then if you drink good wines, they keep the fire going.

I have two categories of wine: Wines that I appreciate academically and want to taste, the kind you want to look at like a statue or a painting or a piece of art. But you wouldn't want to buy it and hang it in your living room. Then there are the wines I cherish that make me long for the corkscrew and another bottle. That is how I see Riesling. That is what I do at Weingut Selbach-Oster.

"I have two categories of wine: Wines that I appreciate academically and want to taste, the kind you want to look at like a statue or a painting or a piece of art. But you wouldn't want to buy it and hang it in your living room. Then there are the wines I cherish that make me long for the corkscrew and another bottle. That is how I see Riesling. That is what I do at Weingut Selbach-Oster."

SELBACH·OSTER

2008

ZELTINGER SONNENUHR RIESLING SPÄTLESE

PRÄDIKATSWEIN · PRODUCT OF GERMANY
GUTSABFÜLLUNG WEINGUT SELBACH-OSTER · D-54492 ZELTINGEN
L - A.P. NR. 2 606 319 018 09 · Enthält Sulfite

Mosel
alc. 7,5% vol · 750 ml e

German wine labels are known for carrying detailed information that includes not only producer and vineyard but also notations about degree of sweetness (*Spätlese*, meaning "late harvest," or made from grapes that are fully ripe and therefore containing more sugar, picked after the normal harvest) and quality level (*Pradikätswein*, or "top quality" wine) as determined by an analysis or A.P. number (*Amtliche Prüfungsnummer*) that is required by law.

THE VINTNER'S GLOSSARY

Aging
Maturation or development of wine over the course of its life in the cellar (typically in oak barrels), or post-bottling.

Appellation
The official name of a wine-growing/winemaking region; can be as large as a country or as small as a geographically defined region such as Bordeaux (France) or Yakima Valley (Washington, U.S.). Usually wineries will use the smallest or most distinct appellation they are entitled to (as in a village or valley vs. a state or country).

Battonage
Stirring the sediments of a wine that is in barrel.

Brett (or *Brettanomyces*)
A fastidious wild yeast known to cause a range of texture, smell, and flavor characteristics in wines.

Cap
A thick layer of grape skins that forms at the top of a fermenting vessel of juice or raw wine; the skins fill with CO_2 from the fermentation and rise to the top.

Cellarmaster
Typically a winery's production manager who works under the winemaker to oversee the cellar crew and carry out all production operations such as processing grapes and bottling.

Chaptalization
The addition of sugar to the grape must for conversion into alcohol during fermentation; often done to increase alcohol content.

Commune
A subregion equating to a town or village, such as Chambolle-Musigny, Burgundy, France.

The crush
The activity immediately after harvest and before fermentation, when grapes are processed (crushed and pressed).

Cuvée
A French wine term generally refering to any specific batch of wine in the cellar, but often used to identify special lots made from a specific vineyard or a particular blend.

Delastage
Separating juice and skins from seeds during fermentation.

Enologist/oenologist
A person trained in the science of wine and winemaking; enologists often work in the laboratory, but may also serve as winemaker.

Enology/oenology
The science and study of all aspects of wine and winemaking (except viticulture).

Enophile/oenophile
A wine enthusiast.

Fermentation
The process that converts the sugar in grape juice into alcohol and CO_2.

Filtering
Using a semi-porous medium to clarify wine before it is bottled and remove any undesirable elements; wine is typically filtered through diatomaceous earth (a naturally occurring sedimentary rock consisting of fossilized remains of diatoms), cellulose pads, or micropore filters fine enough to remove microorganisms.

Fining
Adding a material that combines with certain elements in the wine to clarify and/or improve stability, color, smell, taste, or texture; fining is typically done after fermentation and before bottling.

Free-run juice
Juice that runs off freely, without pressing, after grapes are crushed during the processing stage of winemaking.

Grand Cru
Highest classification of some French appellations.

Green harvest
Cluster thinning; removal of unripe grapes prior to harvest.

Harvest/vendange
The period when ripe grapes are picked and processed.

Hopper
A receiving device that holds grapes for distribution to the stemmer-crusher, or the receiving device that holds corks and releases them to the bottling line corker.

Hose jockey
A cellar worker who does the daily physical work at a winery, such as processing grapes, racking wines, topping up barrels, fining, filtering, and bottling.

Hydrogen sulfide
H_2S, or the compound that is responsible for a rotten egg smell.

Internal "bladder" on the press
An inflatable bag inside a wine press that squeezes the grapes against the inside of the press, causing them to release their juice.

Malolactic fermentation (ML)
A secondary (bacterial) fermentation whereby tart-tasting malic acid present in the wine is converted into softer-tasting lactic acid; ML tends to create a rounder, fuller body, or "mouthfeel," to the wine.

Microorganisms
Yeast and bacteria, some of which have a predictably positive or negative influence on wine.

Must
Crushed grapes (including the juice, pulp, skin, seeds, and stems) before and during fermentation; once the juice is pressed off after fermentation, the solid portion left is called pomace.

Must lines
Hoses and conveyors used for transferring unfermented and fermenting grapes and juice.

Must pump
Pump used for transferring unfermented and fermenting grapes and juice.

Oxidize/oxidation
Exposure to oxygen at any time during a wine's life.

Oxygen reduced
A low-oxygen environment.

Pomace
The solid portion that remains after the must is pressed off, after fermentation.

Premier Cru
French (upper) classification of a given appellation.

Pump-over
Using a pump to wet and submerge the grape skins during fermentation; wine is typically pumped from the bottom of a tank up to the top, where it is sprayed over the cap.

Punch down
Plunging grape skins that have risen to the top of a vessel (forming a cap) down into the liquid level; punching down is done during fermentation when juice is sitting in contact with skin and seeds.

Racking
Transferring or moving wine from one container to another as it is maturing in the cellar between its fermentation and bottling.

Reductive/reduced
Smelling or tasting mildly like H_2S (hydrogen sulfide).

Saignée
Bleeding off the free run juice, immediately after crushing red grapes, to increase the ratio of skins to grape juice; what is bled off in this method is often used for making rosé wines as it has not yet absorbed color from the skins.

Stemmer-crusher
A machine that separates grapes from their stems and gently breaks (or crushes) them without damaging the seeds.

Sulfite
SO_2/Potasium metabisulfite; used to stabilize or preserve wines by inhibiting enzymatic action, serving as an antioxidant, and discouraging or killing microorganisms.

Tannins
Complex chemical compounds (plant-derived polyphenols) derived from the skins, stems, and seeds of grapes (and also new oak barrels); they contribute astringency, bitterness, and structure to wines.

Terroir
All elements that influence a vineyard and contribute to the unique qualities of a crop; terroir is typically used to define characteristics bestowed by geography (rather than man), such as soil, topography, and weather conditions.

Topping up
Using finished wine (from the same lot) to fill tanks or barrels, thereby reducing headspace and oxygen exposure.

Vigneron/winegrower
A person who both grows grapes and makes wine.

Vintage
The year the grape was grown, often indicated on the wine label.

Viticulturist/grape grower
A person who grows grapes (but typically does not make wine).

Winemaker
The visionary responsible for overseeing all aspects of winemaking, from decisions about when and how to pick grapes through production, aging, bottling, and quality.

RESOURCES

PHOTOGRAPHER

Brian Piper
Piper Photography
640 Snyder Ave., Suite L
West Chester, PA 19382
610-344-3955
www.piperphoto.com

CONTRIBUTORS

Alexis Bailly Vineyard
18200 Kirby Avenue
Hastings, MN 55033
651-437-1413
www.abvwines.com

Ed Boyce and Sarah O'Herron
Black Ankle Vineyards
14463 Black Ankle Road
Mt Airy, MD 21771
240- 464-3279
www.blackankle.com

Chaddsford Winery
632 Baltimore Pike
Chadds Ford, PA 19317
610-388-6221
www.chaddsford.com

Mark Chien, Wine Grape Educator
Penn State Cooperative Extension
College of Agricultural Sciences
The Pennsylvania State University
Lancaster, PA
717-394-6851
mlc12@psu.edu

City Winery
143 Varick Street
New York, NY 10013
212-608-0555
www.citywinery.com

Eileen Crane, CEO & Founding Winemaker
Domaine Carneros
1240 Duhig Road
Napa, CA 94559
800-716-2788
www.domainecarneros.com

Crushpad
2573 3rd Street
San Francisco, CA 94107
415-864-4232
www.crushpadwine.com

Peter Gago, Chief Winemaker
Penfolds
77 Southbank Boulevard
Southbank, VIC 3006
Australia
+61 3 9633 2000
www.penfolds.com

Aljoscha Goldschmidt, Farm Director & Enologist
Corzano e Paterno
9 Via San Vito di Sopra
50026 San Casciano in
Val di Pesa FI
Italy
+39 055 8248 179
www.corzanoepaterno.com

Jon Held, General Manager
Stone Hill Winery
1101 Stone Hill Highway
Herman, MO 65041
573-486-2221
800-909-Wine
www.stonehillwinery.com

Inniskillin Wines Inc
1499 Niagara Pkwy, RR#1
Niagara-on-the-Lake,
ON LOS 1 JO Canada
905-468-2187
www.inniskillin.com

Marc Kent, Winemaker
Boekenhoutskloof Winery
P.O. Box 433
Excelsior Road
Franschhoek 7690
South Africa
+27 (0) 21 876 3320
www.boekenhoutskloof.co.za

Keystone Cooperage
1216 Jefferson Road
Jefferson, PA 15344
724-883-4952
www.keystonecooperage.com

Kobrand Corporation
130 East 40th Street
New York, NY 10016
www.kobrandwine.com

Adam Lee, Co-owner & Winemaker
Siduri Winery
980 Airway Court, Suite C
Santa Rosa, CA 95403
707-578-3882
www.siduri.com

Karen and Tony Mangus
Historic Hopewell Vineyard
110 Lower Hopewell Road
Oxford, PA 19363
www.historichopewellvine-yards.com

Aurelio Montes, Chief Winemaker & President
Viña Montes
Av. Del Condor Sur N°590
Huechuraba, Santiago
Chile
(562) 248 4805
www.monteswines.com

Lucie Morton, Viticulturist
P.O. Box 327
Broad Run, VA 20137

Richard Olsen-Harbich, Winemaker
Don Cavaluzzi, Cellarmaster
Raphael
P.O. Box 17
39390 Main Road, Route 25
Peconic, NY 11958
631-765-1100
www.raphaelwine.com

Gary Pisoni, Founder & Visionary
Pisoni Vineyards & Winery
P.O. Box 908
Gonzales, CA 93926 USA
800-270-2525
www.pisonivineyards.com

Johannes Selbach, Owner & Winemaker
Weingut Selbach-Oster
Uferallee 23
54492 Zeltingen, Germany
+49 6532 2081
www.selbach-oster.de

Supreme Corq
5901 S. 226th Street
Kent, Washington 98032
800-794-4160
www.supremecorq.com

Pauline Vauthier, Technical Director
Chateau Ausone
33330 St. Emilion, France
www.chatgeau-ausone-saint-emilion.com

Vineyard Labour Coulee
Castle of La Roche aux Moines
49170 Savennieres
France
0033 (0)2 41 72 22 32
www.coulee-de-serrant.com

Vinquiry Labs
7795 Bell Road
Windsor, CA 95492
707-838-6312
www.vinquiry.com

Kim and Jan Waltz
Waltz Vineyard
1599 Old Line Road
Manheim, PA 17545
www.waltzvineyard@dejazzed
.com

PUBLICATIONS

GRAPE GROWING BOOKS

Clarke, Oz, and Margaret Rand. *Oz Clarke's Encyclopedia of Grapes*. New York: Harcourt, 2001.

Coombe, B. G., P. R. Dry, and T. G. Amos. *Viticulture*. Adelaide: Winetitles, 2001.

Coombe, Bryan George, and P. R. Dry. *Viticulture*. Vol. 2. Adelaide: Winetitles, 1992.

Fanet, Jacques, and Florence Brutton. *Great Wine Terroirs*. Berkeley: University of California, 2004.

Galet, Pierre. *A Practical Ampelography: Grapevine Identification*. Ithaca, N.Y.: Comstock Pub. Associates, 1979.

Hellman, Edward W. *Oregon Viticulture*. Corvallis: Oregon State UP, 2003.

Isaacs, Rufus, and Mary Louise Flint. *A Pocket Guide for Grape IPM Scouting in the North Central and Eastern U.S.* East Lansing, MI: Michigan State University Extension, 2007.

Law, Jim. *The Backyard Vintner: An Enthusiast's Guide to Growing Grapes and Making Wine at Home*. Beverly, MA: Quarry, 2005.

Mullins, Michael G., Alain Bouquet, and Larry E. Williams. *The Biology of the Grapevine*. Cambridge: Cambridge UP, 2007.

Plocher, Thomas A., and Bob Parke. *Northern Winework: Growing Grapes and Making Wine in Cold Climates*. Hugo, MN: Northern Winework, 2001.

Robinson, Jancis. *Vines, Grapes, and Wines*. London: Mitchell Beazley, 2002.

Smart, Richard, and Mike Robinson. *Sunlight into Wine: a Handbook for Wine Grape Canopy Management*. Adelaide: Winetitles, 2006.

White, R. E. *Soils for Fine Wines*. New York: Oxford UP, 2003.

Wilson, James E. *Terroir: the Role of Geology, Climate, and Culture in the Making of French Wines*. London: Mitchell Beazley, 1998.

Winkler, A. J., James A. Cook, W. M. Kliewer, and Lloyd A. Lider. *General Viticulture*. Berkeley: University of California, 1974.

Wolf, Tony Kenneth. *Wine Grape Production Guide for Eastern North America*. Ithaca, N.Y.: Natural Resource, Agriculture, and Engineering Service (NRAES) Cooperative Extension, 2008.

Zabadal, Thomas J., and Jeffrey A. Andresen. *Vineyard Establishment*. East Lansing, MI: Michigan State University Extension, 1997.

WINEMAKING BOOKS:

Boulton, Roger B., Vernon L. Singleton, Linda F. Bisson, and Ralph E. Kunkee. *Principles and Practices of Winemaking*. New York: Springer, 1999.

Fugelsang, K. C., and Charles G. Edwards. *Wine Microbiology*. New York, NY: Springer, 2007.

Goode, Jamie. *The Science of Wine: From Vine to Glass*. Berkeley: University of California, 2006.

Johnson, Hugh, and Jancis Robinson. *The World Atlas of Wine*. London: Mitchell Beazley, 2007.

Peynaud, Emile. *Knowing and Making Wine*. New York: J. Wiley, 1984.

Robinson, Jancis. *The Oxford Companion to Wine*. Oxford: Oxford UP, 2006.

Zoecklein, Bruce W., Kenneth C. Fugelsang, Barry H. Gump, and Fred S. Nury. *Wine Analysis and Production*. New York: Kluwer, 1999.

TRADE JOURNALS

PWV Incorporated. *Practical Winery and Vineyard*. www.practicalwinery.com

Vineyard & Winery Management, Inc. *Vineyard & Winery Management Magazine*. www.vwm-online.com

Wine Communications Group. "Wine Business Monthly." *Wine Business* 2010. www.winebusiness.com

Winetitles Pty Ltd. "Australian & New Zealand Grapegrower and Winemaker." *Winebiz / The Australian & New Zealand Grapegrower & Winemaker*. 1995. www.grapeandwine.com.au

Winetitles Pty Ltd. "Australian & New Zealand Wine Industry Journal." *Winetitles—Specialist Publishers to the Grape and Wine Industry*. 1995. www.winetitles.com.au/wij/about.asp

Winter, Erika, John Whiting, and Jacques Rousseau. *Winegrape Berry Sensory Assessment in Australia*. Adelaide: Winetitles, 2004.

CONSUMER WINE PUBLICATIONS

Wine Spectator. M. Shanken Communications. www.winespectator.com

The Wine Appreciation Guild Online. www.wineappreciation.com

Wine Enthusiast Magazine / Wine Ratings, Reviews, Buying Guide, 101 Info, Food Pairings, Recipes, Blogs. www.winemag.com

Wine News, Wine Recommendations, Wine Competitions, Wine Tastings, Wine Vintages, Learn about Wine, Decanter Magazine — Decanter.com. IPC Media Limited. www.decanter.com

PROFESSIONAL WINE-RELATED RESOURCES

Cornell University
Ithaca, New York, USA
www.nysaes.cornell.edu

Geisenheim University
Germany, Dekanat of Drawer
STR. 1
65366 Geisenheim
06722 - 502,714
geisenheim.hs-rm.de

Istituto di Frutti
Viticoltura, Piacenza, Italy
www.unicatt.it/ucsc

Université de Bourgogne
Erasme Esplanade BP 27877 -
21078 Dijon Cedex
03 80 39 50 00
www.u-bourgogne.fr

Universite de Montpellier
France
www.univ-montp2.fr
Institut Universitaire de la
Vigne et du Vin

University of Adelaide
Australia, SA 5005 Australia
+61 8 8303 4455
www.usc.adelaide.edu.au/
asistm/winemaking/

**University of California at Davis
Viticulture & Enology
Department**
Davis, California, USA
530-752-0380
www.wineserver.ucdavis.edu

**Washington State University,
Viticulture & Enology
Department**
Pullman, Washington
509-335-9502
www.wineeducation.wsu.edu

WINE LIFESTYLE RESOURCES

American Wine Society
Durham, North Carolina, USA
919-403-0022
www.americanwinesociety.org

Society of Wine Educators
Washington, DC USA
202-408-8777
www.societyofwineeducators.org

Wine Tasters Guild
1515 Michigan N. E.
Grand Rapids, MI 49503
616-454-7518
www.tastersguild.com

WINEMAKING SUPPLIES AND EQUIPMENT:

Art of Brewing
Chessington, Surrey, U.K.
020 8397 2111
www.art-of-brewing.co.uk

The Compleat Winemaker
Saint Helena, CA 94574
707-963-9681
www.tcw-web.com

Crosby and Baker Ltd.,
999 Main Road
Westport, MA 02790
508-636-5154
www.crosby-baker.com

E.C. Kraus
Independence
MO 64054
816-254-7448
www.ECKraus.com

Francois Frères Barrels
21190 Saint Romain, France
03 80 21 23 33
www.francoisfreres.com

G. W. Kent, Inc.
506 S. Huron
Ypsilanti, MI 48197
800-333-4288
www.gwkent.com

Lallemand Company
(See Scott Laboratories)
www.lallemandwine.us

Presque Isle Wine Cellars
9440 West Main Road
North East, PA 16428
800-488-7492
www.piwine.com

Prospero Equipment Corp.
123 Castleton Street
Pleasantville, NY 10570
www.prosperocorp.biz

Scott Laboratories, Inc.
950 Brock Road South, Unit 1
Pickering, ON L1W2A1
Canada
www.scottlab.com

Winequip
59 Banbury Road Reservoir
Melbourne
03 9462 4777
www.winequip.com.au

VINEYARD SUPPLIES

Cameron & Cameron
1175 River Road
Fulton, CA 95439
800-546-7706
www.ccivineyard.com

Growers Supply Center
2415 Harford Road
Fallston, MD 21047
410-931-3111

H and W Equipment
RR# 2, 827 Line 4
Niagara on the Lake, ON
LOS 1J0 Canada
905-468-5016
www.vineyardmachines.com

Orchard Valley Supply
Harrisburgh, NC
888-755-0098
www.orchardvalleysupply.com

Ryset Australia
30 Kolora Road
Heidelberg West Victoria, 3081
Australia
(03) 9457 2982

Spec Trellising
39 Indian Drive
Warminster, PA 18974
800-237-4594
www.spectrellising.com

GRAPEVINE NURSERIES

Domaine de Rochecorbiere
Janine et Alain Bidon
69380 Chessy, France
+33 (0)4 78 43 92 34

Double A Vineyards
10277 Christy Road
Fredonia, NY 14063
716-672-8493
www.rakgrape.com

**Lincoln Peak Vineyard and
Nursery**
142 River Road
New Haven, VT 05472
802-388-7368
www.lincolnpeakvineyard.com

Mori Vines Inc.
Oliver, British Columbia,
Canada
250-498-3350
www.morivines.com

Novavine Grapevine Nursery
6735 Sonoma Highway
Santa Rosa, CA 95409
707-539-5678
www.novavine.com

Pepinieres Martin Viticole
Vaucluse, France
pepinieres.martin@wanadoo.fr

Vintage Nursery
27920 McCombs Avenue
Wasco, CA 93280
661-758-4777
www.vintagenurseries.com

GRAPE AND JUICE SUPPLIERS

Crushpad
3105 Silverado Trail
Napa, CA 94558
707-637-8821
www.crushpadwine.com

Walkers Fruit Basket and Press House
RR 39
Fredonia, NY, 14062
716-679-1292

Your Local Fresh Market
Some of the most convenient grape resources are the fresh markets in major cities where Northern hemisphere wine grapes come in Sepember and October and Southern hemisphere grapes arrive in March and April.
Fax (509)782-1203
info@wawgg.org

PHOTOGRAPHY CREDITS

INDEX

ACKNOWLEDGMENTS

ABOUT THE AUTHOR

Eric Miller spent a good portion of his youth growing up in Europe, including a small village in Burgundy, where he first developed his passion for wine. When his family returned to the United States in 1970, they established Benmarl Vineyards in the Hudson Valley, holder of New York State's Farm Winery License #1. After doing his early vineyard and wine experimentation in New York, Eric and his wife Lee founded the Chaddsford Winery in southeastern Pennsylvania's Brandywine Valley in 1982, joining a few other pioneers in developing Pennsylvania's fledgling wine industry. Since then, Chaddsford has grown to become Pennsylvania's largest winery, and Eric Miller is among a handful of East Coast United States winemakers who have achieved national acclaim and recognition. His wines have been called "enchanting" and "perfect" by *Gourmet*, and have been featured in *Food & Wine*, *The New York Times*, *Decanter*, *The Robb Report*, and many other prestigious wine and food publications.

Every wine has a soul, and for as long as I can remember, I have struggled with an addiction not only to understand its complex nature, but to explain it. Alas, it would be a confusing mess to read about it in these pages if it weren't for my life companion and co-author on this book, Lee Miller. Lee is one of those rare people who have the ability to see the whole picture, understand the whole process, taste all the flavors of something, and distill the matter down to its few key points. In the course of writing this book, Lee has called me a "creative writer" as she patiently redirected and edited my work and convinced me of what I meant to say. Her name really should be before mine as author, except I know a little more about growing wine than she does.

I also want to acknowledge the dogged work of Russell Burda, who collected and secured reproduction rights for what is the most striking collection of wine photos I have ever seen. Without Russ, this book would not have become so comfortable on the coffee table. And my heartfelt thanks to the very generous Mark Chien, Penn State Cooperative Extension viticulturlist, who not only shared many photos from his collection, but read and proofed my grape-growing chapters. And finally, I am deeply grateful to my son, Eric Stauffer, UC Davis Class of 2007, for taking the time to review the winemaking selections of this book for technical faux pas, because it will save me embarrassment and has been another excuse for us to talk about making wine.